ULTIMATE
VEGETARIAN
COOKBOOK

ULTIMATE
VEGETARIAN
COOKBOOK

PAUL GAYLER

Photography by Philip Wilkins

A DK PUBLISHING BOOK

www.dk.com

A DK PUBLISHING BOOK
www.dk.com

*For the new-age vegetarians who
demand quality, taste, and innovation*

Project Editor Jo Younger

US Editors Iris Rosoff, Joan Whitman

Art Editor Julia Worth

Editor Nicky Vimpany

Designer Laura Jackson

DTP Designer Bridget Roseberry

Senior Managing Editor Krystyna Mayer

Deputy Art Director Carole Ash

Production Manager Maryann Webster

Home Economist Jane Suthering

First American Edition 1999
4 6 8 10 9 7 5 3

Published in the United States by
DK Publishing, Inc.
95 Madison Avenue
New York, New York 10016

Copyright © 1999 Dorling Kindersley Limited, London
Text copyright © 1999 Paul Gayler

Library of Congress Cataloging-in-Publication Data

Gayler, Paul.
    Ultimate Vegetarian / by Paul Gayler. -- 1st American ed.
       p. cm.
    Includes index.
    ISBN 0–7894–4184–5 (alk. paper)
    1. Vegetarian cookery. I. Title.
TX837.G36 1999
641.5'636--dc21   98-37317
                CIP

Reproduced by GRB Editrice, Verona
Printed and bound in Hong Kong by Dai Nippon

POINTS TO REMEMBER

All spoon measurements are level unless otherwise stated. Follow either
metric or imperial measurements, never mix the two. Eggs are medium
unless otherwise stated. Milk is regular milk unless otherwise stated. The
nutritional notes give values per portion and are an estimate only, based
on average values. For convection ovens, temperatures should be adjusted
according to the manufacturer's instructions. Some of the cheeses in this
book may be made with animal rennet. Strict vegetarians may wish to
substitute cheeses made with vegetarian rennet where appropriate.

CONTENTS

GALLERY

*A visual preview of versatile vegetarian
cuisine, from sophisticated soups and
stuffed vegetables through tarts and pies to
shamelessly indulgent desserts.*

INGREDIENTS

A guide to all the essential basic ingredients for the modern vegetarian cook plus a few exotic extras to spice up your repertoire, with information on choosing, storing, and cooking.

EQUIPMENT & TECHNIQUES

How to choose and use equipment for vegetarian cooking, plus a step-by-step guide to all the essential basic techniques.

RECIPES

Over 140 creative and delicious recipes to suit any occasion, with influences from every corner of the globe, which will inspire everyone who loves good food.

INTRODUCTION

IT IS NEARLY 15 YEARS since I devised my first vegetarian menu and offered it alongside the conventional one at Inigo Jones, the London restaurant where I worked as chef director. At that time, vegetarianism and *haute cuisine* were considered two culinary extremes, never destined to meet on the same plate. Today the tables have turned, and it is rare to find a restaurant that does not include a vegetarian option on its menu. Over the last decade there has been a quiet revolution in the way we eat: traditional meal structures have broken down; ingredients that were once considered exotic are now commonplace; and vegetarian food has been accepted as part of the mainstream.

THE MODERN VEGETARIAN

Leaf through the vegetarian cookbooks of 20 years ago and you will find a depressing list of worthy, but dull culinary staples: whole wheat flour, brown rice, lentils, root vegetables, and lots of nuts. These were served in relentlessly heavy and unpalatable combinations with nothing to relieve them. Nowadays, many vegetarian staples have been taken up by chefs and cookbook writers, with spectacular results. Lentils, for example, are wildly fashionable, particularly the tiny, slate-blue baby lentils from France. These are combined with sophisticated flavorings such as balsamic vinegar, herbs, and truffles. Root vegetables are roasted to bring out their natural sweetness or mixed to a rich, smooth puree with cream or olive oil. Substitute ingredients such as margarine and carob are being dropped and replaced by the real thing. After all, why shouldn't vegetarians enjoy good butter and quality chocolate? I'm more interested in creating sophisticated vegetarian food that has depth of flavor. This isn't difficult to achieve. Dried mushrooms and tomato concentrates, Asian seasonings such as soy sauce, high-quality olive oils, and various cooking pastes such as tapenade and harissa, are staples in the modern kitchen, and all of these are appropriate ingredients for vegetarian recipes.

THE GLOBAL KITCHEN

The dazzling array of ingredients now available from all over the world has led to an explosion of interest in cooking. The fact that we can go into supermarkets now and pick up Asian herbs alongside French dairy products and Mexican salsas has made us all into culinary artists, mixing and matching cooking styles and ingredients. Done with restraint and a respect for flavors, this innovative way of eating can be incredibly exciting. It has opened up a whole new world of vegetarian cuisine in which Spanish gazpacho can be flavored with mild spices, pesto can be made with goat cheese, and risotto can be flavored with Thai ingredients such as lemongrass, coconut, and cilantro.

COOKING FOR THE FUTURE

I find that vegetarian food works best if you concentrate on providing a harmonious balance of flavors, textures, and colors. Although you can still cook a main dish if that is how you like to eat, it is often easier and more appropriate to prepare a selection of lighter dishes. This way of eating is nothing new in the Middle East, India, and the Far East, and I find these cuisines a continual source of inspiration. My cooking has not been immune to the Mediterranean fever that has swept the culinary world either. Mediterranean influences are here to stay, and the food of Italy, in particular, has had a lasting impact on the way we eat. This is great news for vegetarians, for surely no other nation has created as many imaginative vegetable dishes as Italy, not to mention all the meatless pasta sauces and risottos. Unlike Italian cooking, French cuisine is not rich in vegetarian dishes. However, I believe that classic French cooking techniques can be applied to an exciting range of global ingredients, giving a new refinement to vegetarian cooking. In devising recipes for this book, I have been able to experiment with the pick of the best produce from all over the world. Whether you are a committed vegetarian or a confirmed carnivore, I think you will be as gratified as I was to discover how diverse and exciting modern vegetarian cooking can be. From Mardi Gras Jambalaya to Parsnip and Wild Rice Mulligatawny, Asian Noodle Salad to Tuscan Roll, I hope this book has something to delight anyone who loves good food.

GALLERY

THIS INSPIRATIONAL GALLERY OF VEGETARIAN DISHES

IS DESIGNED TO TANTALIZE EVERY SENSE:

STUFFED VEGETABLES OOZING WITH FLAVOR, ALFRESCO

FOOD SIZZLING OVER HOT COALS, LUSCIOUS DESSERTS

DRIPPING WITH FRUIT, AND SO MUCH MORE. USE THESE PAGES

TO GET A TASTE OF THE TREATS THAT LIE IN STORE IN

THE RECIPE SECTION, OR TO PLAN A MENU TO TEMPT YOUR

FRIENDS OR INDULGE YOURSELF.

SOUPS

BECAUSE SOUPS CAN BE PREPARED well in advance, they are ideal for serving at dinner parties, for special occasions, or for quick lunches. Presentation is all important. With a few garnishes you can transform a soup into something special. Whether it is a light, cold consommé or a more warming brew, soup can make an impressive start to a meal, or be a complete meal in itself.

"It's good soup and not fine words that keeps me alive."

Molière, playwright, 1672

Above and opposite
CHILLED CUCUMBER &
BULGUR SOUP *(see page 65)*

PARSNIP & WILD RICE
MULLIGATAWNY
(see page 61)

EARLY
SUMMER
BASIL SOUP
(see page 60)

here are soups for all seasons — satisfying winter warmers or

Refreshing, cool, smooth summer revivers

CHICKPEA & SWISS CHARD
MINESTRONE WITH PESTO
(see page 60)

STUFFED VEGETABLES

Above and opposite
STUFFED GOLDEN & RED
PEPPERS *(see page 113)*

THERE IS SOMETHING very satisfying about preparing vegetables to be stuffed, and the process is relatively simple, too. Stuffings can consist of just a few carefully chosen ingredients simply thrown together, or they can be more elaborate and prepared with greater care for more sumptuous effects. Whatever the aim — a quick and simple light lunch or a dinner party show-stopper — I hope these recipes will provide the inspiration.

"... Taste the fruit and resign yourself to the influences of each."

Henry David Thoreau, essayist, naturalist, and poet, 1817–1862

ASIAN
STUFFED
EGGPLANT
(see page 110)

GEM SQUASH
WITH TOFU
(see page 108)

STUFFED
ROASTED
ONIONS
(see page 111)

Dramatic centerpieces, these vegetables are bursting with flavor

ALFRESCO FOOD

COOKING IN THE FRESH AIR over hot coals imparts a delicious smoky taste to food. With a little imagination you can produce an impressive vegetarian barbecue spread. Here, succulent vegetables and spicy marinades and juicy chunks of fruit infused with the subtle taste of lemongrass are combined with the charcoal-grilled flavors of spiced corn and aromatic herby tomatoes.

"A man hath no better thing under the sun, than to eat, and to drink, and to be merry."

Ecclesiastes, Old Testament, 977 BC

Above and opposite
HOT CHILI-BASTED CORN ON THE COB *(see page 150)*

Succulent vegetables and luscious fruit, simply chargrilled, tease the senses

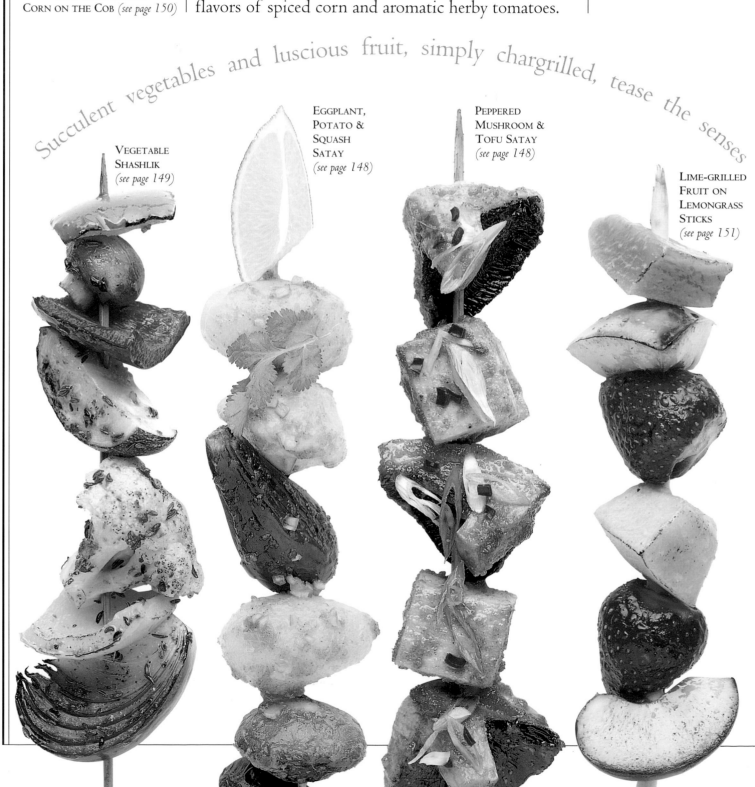

VEGETABLE SHASHLIK
(see page 149)

EGGPLANT, POTATO & SQUASH SATAY
(see page 148)

PEPPERED MUSHROOM & TOFU SATAY
(see page 148)

LIME-GRILLED FRUIT ON LEMONGRASS STICKS
(see page 151)

TARTS & PIES

CRISP, DELICATE PASTRY makes a perfect wrapping for an infinite variety of fillings. Here, I have built up high-rise pies that slice open to reveal colorful layers of ingredients, and I have created delicious fillings for delicate phyllo pastry and intriguing pastry creations that are impressive enough for a celebratory meal. There are pastries for picnics as well as dinners and parties.

"What is a roofless cathedral compared to a well-built pie?"

William Maginn, poet, 1794–1842

Above and opposite
CEPE, WALNUT & JERUSALEM ARTICHOKE PACKAGES *(see page 73)*

SPINACH, BASIL & PUMPKIN RICE TORTE *(see page 68)*

HIGH-RISE PASTA PIE *(see page 71)*

CARROT & BEAN PIE WITH THYME CREAM *(see page 152)*

Light and crisp pastry, filled with colorful layers of exciting flavors

STACKS

THESE STACKS ARE PILED HIGH with flavor. Here, two appetizers, a salad, and a main course have all been built up using ingredients with contrasting colors and textures, and with the flavors of the Orient, Mediterranean, and Middle East. The recipes are simple to follow and, with a little patience, these gastronomic sculptures are easy to achieve. Flourishes of greens add the finishing touches.

"If one has the art, then a piece of celery or salted cabbage can be made into a marvelous delicacy."

Yuan Mei, Chinese poet, 18th century

Above and opposite
CAPONATA ON ROASTED GARLIC
BRUSCHETTA *(see page 50)*

STACKED VEGETABLE
CEVICHE *(see page 54)*

TOASTED MILLET &
CUMIN VEGETABLES
(see page 103)

The art of presentation reaches new heights: these culinary creations are truly gastronomic treats

SINGAPORE
NOODLE SALAD
(see page 120)

DESSERTS

Above and opposite
**HAZELNUT TORTE WITH
KIRSCH & BLUEBERRIES**
(see page 126)

EVERYONE LOVES DESSERTS. I have included recipes
for unusual, sweet, vegetable desserts; more conventional
crème caramels; and crisp, refreshing ices. Some recipes
are simple to prepare, and others need a little more
time and attention to achieve the end result. I have tried
to incorporate a selection of desserts to suit every taste,
making full use of the diversity of ingredients available.

*"I like to shock people —
especially with dessert. If you
really know the classics, then
you can vary as you like."*

Charles Palmer, chef,
20th century

**FROZEN LEMON YOGURT
& PEPPER CHERRIES**
(see page 133)

**ITALIAN CREME
CARAMEL**
(see page 135)

Mouthwatering desserts with cascades of fruit and pools of sauce dazzle the eye

**BUTTERNUT SOUFFLE WITH
BLACKBERRIES** *(see page 131)*

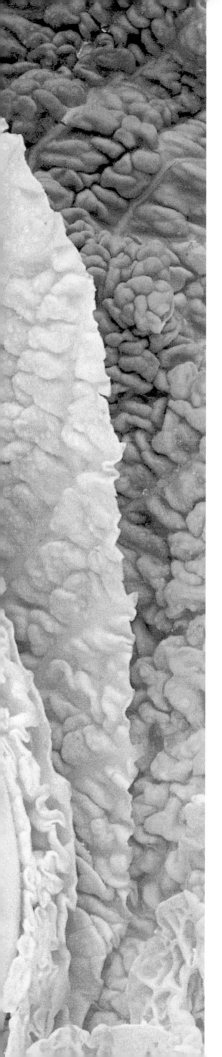

INGREDIENTS

HERE IS AN ILLUSTRATED GUIDE TO THE CORNUCOPIA

OF FRESH INGREDIENTS AVAILABLE TO VEGETARIANS TODAY,

WITH ADVICE ON SELECTION, STORAGE, AND

PREPARATION. ALL FRESH PRODUCE IS AT ITS BEST EATEN AS

SOON AS POSSIBLE AFTER PURCHASE, SO MAKE THE

MOST OF LOCAL STORES, FARMERS' MARKETS, AND

DELICATESSENS. BUY SMALL AMOUNTS OFTEN RATHER

THAN KEEPING INGREDIENTS FOR A LONG TIME.

SHOOTS, PODS & SEEDS

PODS AND SEEDS are packed with nutrients and provide protein and fiber. Shoots contain small amounts of vitamins and add wonderful flavor and texture to dishes.

FENNEL has a lovely, sweet, aniseed flavor. Buy plump bulbs. After cutting, drop them into water with a little lemon juice to prevent discoloring.

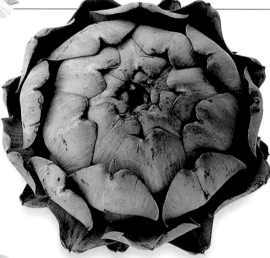

ARTICHOKES are a real treat, well worth the trouble they take to prepare. They have a subtle, earthy flavor and can be boiled or baked. Serve them hot or cold.

ASPARAGUS should have tight buds and tender stems. Cook them in a bundle, standing in 1 inch (2.5cm) of water. Cover with foil to keep the steam in.

CELERY stalks should snap easily; soft stalks indicate the celery is past its prime. It is excellent raw in salads, and with dips or cheese, and can be braised or used in soups and stocks.

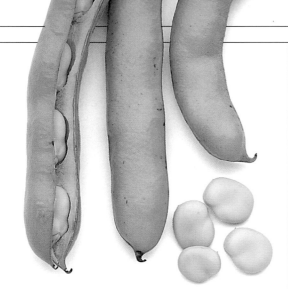

FAVA BEANS, snipped at both ends, can be eaten in the pod when young and tender. If they are tougher, remove from the pods, cook in boiling water, and rub off the skins.

OKRA is pungent and slightly glutinous. Buy pods that will snap, not bend, and trim the stalks before cooking. Okra is good in most stews, curries, and rice dishes.

BABY CORN comes from the same plant as regular corn, but is picked young. It is excellent in stir-fries; add it whole or cut in half lengthwise and cook for just a few minutes.

CORN is best soon after picking. Look for creamy, tightly packed kernels. Strip off the husks and boil or barbecue; do not add salt since it will toughen the kernels.

SNOW PEAS are immature peas that are eaten complete with the pod. Bright, flat, fresh-looking pods with slight swellings are best. Cook briefly in boiling water or stir-fry.

FRESH PEAS are more widely available than they used to be; the pods should be bright and full, but not hard. Pop peas out of the pods and cook briefly in boiling water.

LEAFY GREENS

GREEN LEAFY VEGETABLES contain valuable amounts of vitamins A, B, and C, as well as fiber, iron, and calcium. They keep well for about three days in the salad drawer of the refrigerator. Serve greens raw or lightly cooked to preserve their nutrients.

BOK CHOY has a delicate, mild flavor and is used in many Asian dishes. For the best results, stir-fry or steam bok choy for the shortest possible time.

KOHLRABI is crisp with a nutty flavor. Buy the smallest you can find; the youngest can be sliced and stir-fried, otherwise steam for 15–20 minutes, then peel.

NAPA is a succulent cabbage with a delicate flavor. It is excellent in stir-fries and soups as well as raw. It keeps for about a week in the refrigerator.

SAVOY CABBAGE is packed with flavor. Look for a firm cabbage with crisp leaves that are dark outside and paler inside. It is delicious cooked slowly with a little butter.

SWISS OR RED CHARD *is delicate and distinctive enough to serve on its own like asparagus. Choose young, tender leaves and steam them lightly to retain their flavor.*

RADICCHIO *is popular for adding color and texture to salads, although it can also be cooked. It has a slightly bitter flavor. Buy bright, crisp, unblemished leaves.*

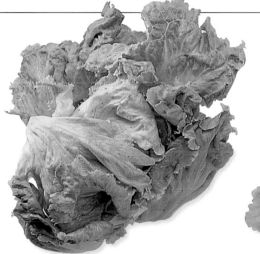

ESCAROLE *is a broad-leaved endive with a characteristic, slightly bitter flavor. The leaves are either pale green or red-tinged and make an interesting addition to salads.*

ARUGULA *has a distinctive, peppery taste and can be added to salads or stirred into pasta sauces. Select bright leaves with no yellowing.*

BELGIAN ENDIVE *is sometimes called chicory or witloof. Look for tightly packed leaves and break them apart to use in salads, braise whole, or serve hot with a cheese sauce.*

CURLY ENDIVE OR FRISEE *is a slightly bitter salad leaf that is both decorative and tasty. Buy with a crisp, light green central core and use as fresh as possible.*

FRUIT VEGETABLES & SQUASH

PEPPERS AND TOMATOES contain more vitamin C than many fruits, and squash contain useful amounts of vitamin A. Fruit vegetables should be stored in the refrigerator, while squash will keep well in a cool place.

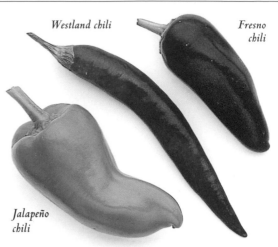

Westland chili

Fresno chili

Jalapeño chili

CHILIES *are available in different colors, shapes, and sizes. As a rule, the smaller the chili, the hotter it is. Protect your hands when handling chilies to avoid irritation.*

Plum tomato

Vine tomatoes

Yellow cherry tomatoes

Red tomato

TOMATOES, *whether red or yellow, should be firm, bright, and plump. Plum tomatoes have the sweetest, most intense flavor and are particularly good for sauces.*

EGGPLANTS *should have a green stalk and be shiny and plump, with no wrinkles or bruises. They can be stuffed, cooked in casseroles, stews, and bakes, or pureed for dips.*

PEPPERS *are available in many colors. Red, yellow, and orange varieties are sweeter than green ones. Use peppers in stir-fries and salads, or try stuffing or roasting them.*

CHAYOTES *have a bland taste that complements stronger flavors. Choose the smallest ones you can find. They can sbe boiled, baked, fried, or stuffed.*

GEM SQUASH *are excellent for individual servings and can be stuffed and roasted. Alternatively, dice the flesh and use it in the same way as that of any other squash.*

BUTTERNUT SQUASH *have a rich, buttery flavor that gives them their name. Choose firm, unblemished specimens, and use them in casseroles, soups, stews, and purees.*

PUMPKIN *is the most familiar of the squash family. Buy small whole ones in preference to slices.*

ONIONS & MUSHROOMS

ONIONS are familiar ingredients that can help protect against heart disease by lowering cholesterol. Wild mushrooms are less familiar, but are now becoming more readily available. They have a delicious flavor and are an important source of B vitamins for vegetarians.

GARLIC is an indispensable flavoring that can be added to many dishes, and is also delicious roasted and served whole. Choose firm, fat bulbs with no sign of shoots.

RED ONIONS are milder and sweeter than most brown varieties, and they are delicious served raw in salads. They retain their color well, even when cooked.

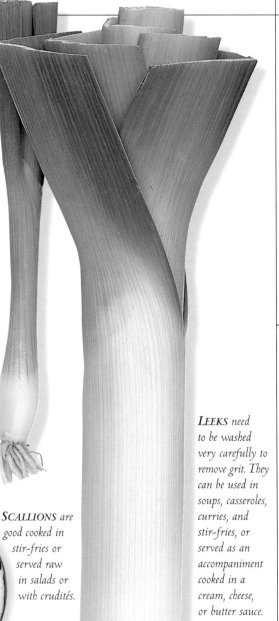

LEEKS need to be washed very carefully to remove grit. They can be used in soups, casseroles, curries, and stir-fries, or served as an accompaniment cooked in a cream, cheese, or butter sauce.

SCALLIONS are good cooked in stir-fries or served raw in salads or with crudités.

ONIONS vary in strength. Generally, the larger the onion, the milder the taste.

SHALLOTS are small, sweet onions, with a more delicate flavor than large onions.

OPEN-CUP MUSHROOMS *are cultivated mushrooms at a fairly late stage of development, when they are fully open. They are the ideal size for stuffing and baking.*

CHANTERELLES *are one of the most attractive mushrooms. Brush and rinse them, then cook gently in butter and cream to prevent toughening, or add to casseroles.*

SHIITAKE MUSHROOMS *should simply be wiped with paper towel before slicing, frying, and adding to rice dishes or stews. They are available fresh and dried.*

OYSTER MUSHROOMS *should be torn into long strips, or used whole if small. They have a strong flavor and a firm texture, and are good in casseroles and Asian dishes.*

CEPES *are one of the tastiest mushrooms available, with a deep, rich flavor. Add a few to cultivated mushroom dishes to intensify the flavor. Porcini are dried cepes.*

MORELS *have a distinctive look and a strong, meaty taste and smell. Wash them well in salty water to remove dirt from the caps. They are available fresh and dried.*

HERBS & SPICES

FRESH HERBS really bring an extra dimension to many dishes. They should be used as soon as possible after buying or picking since they deteriorate quickly. Buy spices in small quantities and, where possible, buy them whole, then grind them yourself for the best flavor.

PARSLEY is available in two varieties, flat-leaf and curly. Flat-leaf parsley has a finer, more robust flavor than curly parsley. Both are used widely to add taste to many dishes.

BASIL blends well with tomatoes and garlic. Its delicate leaves should be treated with care to prevent bruising, and are usually added to dishes at the end of the cooking time.

THYME is particularly pungent when fresh, and aids the digestion of fatty foods. It is a popular addition to bouquet garni, and is robust enough to withstand long, slow cooking.

CILANTRO has a fresh, citrus-like aroma and taste, and is very popular in Asian and Mexican cooking. It can be used with chilies or yogurt in chutneys, relishes, and salsas.

MINT has a distinctive, refreshing flavor and can help digestion. This versatile herb can be combined with sweet or savory ingredients and is delicious with chocolate.

CAYENNE is made from one of the hottest varieties of chili. It is used to give heat to sauces, curries, and stews.

CRUSHED RED PEPPER FLAKES are crushed, dried chilies including the seeds. They are very hot, so use with caution.

PAPRIKA is sweet and mild, with a subtle, peppery taste. It gives warmth and color to stews and sauces.

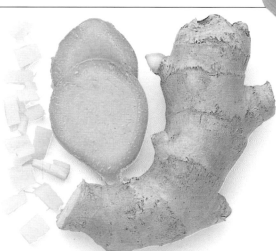

CINNAMON is a warm, fragrant spice used in sweet and savory dishes.

LEMONGRASS has a fresh citrus scent and is popular in Thai dishes.

FRESH GINGER has a spicy, lemony taste, which is far superior to that of dried ginger. It is most often used in Asian and Indian curries and in sweet dishes.

CLOVES are sweet and highly aromatic. They go very well with fruit.

NUTMEG has a warm, pungent flavor, and is best used freshly grated.

STAR ANISE imparts a sweet, aniseed aroma and looks attractive.

SAFFRON is aromatic and tastes slightly bitter. It is often used in rice dishes.

EQUIPMENT
&
TECHNIQUES

ANY ARTIST NEEDS GOOD TOOLS AND SOUND WORKING

PRACTICES, AND A COOK IS NO EXCEPTION. CHOOSING

EQUIPMENT CAREFULLY AND FOLLOWING A FEW BASIC RULES

FOR PREPARING AND COOKING INGREDIENTS CAN REALLY

MAKE A DIFFERENCE TO A RECIPE. THE FOLLOWING PAGES

PROVIDE A VISUAL CATALOG OF THE MOST USEFUL

EQUIPMENT AND TECHNIQUES FOR A VEGETARIAN COOK.

EQUIPMENT

THERE IS AN ENORMOUS RANGE of kitchen equipment available and it can be difficult to know what you really need. Here are some of the things that a vegetarian cook will find most useful. You do not need a lot of equipment, just buy the best quality you can – your cooking will benefit, and you will find that preparation will be much quicker and easier. If you keep your equipment scrupulously clean and dry and your knives sharp, and store everything carefully, these tools should last you a lifetime.

SLOTTED SPOON *This holed spoon is indispensable for skimming stocks and sauces, and for lifting solid food from boiling liquid.*

VEGETABLE PEELER *A good peeler will shave a thinner layer of skin than a knife and so preserve more nutrients.*

LADLE *A ladle is useful for serving soups and stews, and for measuring out batter for making pancakes.*

GARLIC CRUSHER *Easier to use than a knife for crushing garlic, a garlic crusher should ideally have a detachable grill for easy cleaning.*

DARIOLE MOLD *These small, deep-sided molds are used for shaping pastries, desserts, rice, and noodles.*

TARTLET PAN *These pans are ideal for making individual tarts or quiches. The best are nonstick ones.*

RAMEKIN *Individual servings can be brought straight from the oven to the table in these small ceramic dishes.*

SKEWERS *Metal or bamboo skewers can be used to skewer vegetables for barbecuing, and to prick cakes and pies to test for doneness.*

BAKING SHEET *A baking sheet should be sturdy and should not bend in your hand. A nonstick surface is useful, but not essential.*

ROASTING PAN *A good-quality, nonstick roasting pan has many uses, from roasting vegetables to setting polenta.*

SPRINGFORM CAKE PAN *This loose-bottomed pan is useful for delicate cakes and can also be used for raised pies.*

CHOPPING BOARD *A wooden board is kinder to knives than other surfaces. It should never be soaked or submerged in water.*

CHEF'S KNIFE *A chef's knife is indispensable for chopping. It should be well balanced with a deep, curved blade.*

PARING KNIFE *Used for paring, peeling, and scraping, a paring knife should be light, with a handle that is comfortable to hold.*

SAUCEPAN *It is well worth investing in good pots. A stainless steel pot is durable and easy to clean, but look for one that has copper or aluminum sandwiched into the base to help conduct heat evenly.*

FRYING PAN *A large, nonstick, heavy-bottomed pan with sloping sides is the best all-around choice. Use it for sautéeing vegetables and cooking omelettes and pancakes.*

SIEVE *A sieve has a multitude of uses, from sifting flour to straining stocks and soups and pureeing fruit. The best sieves are made from stainless steel, which does not corrode.*

KITCHEN GADGETS

BLENDER *Ingredients for soups, dips, sauces, and drinks can be pureed in a blender.*

FOOD PROCESSOR *This does the job of a blender plus much more. Different blades can chop, mix, grate, and shred.*

HAND-HELD BLENDER *This hand-held blender is useful for pureeing food in a pot. It is compact and saves on storage space and cleaning up — always a bonus.*

PASTA MACHINE *These useful machines roll pasta dough out thinly, kneading it as they do so. The best ones are made of chrome-plated steel.*

TECHNIQUES

PREPARING INGREDIENTS in the correct way ensures the best results and helps cut down on preparation time. These simple techniques show how to get the best from ingredients with a minimum of fuss and waste. Always keep your utensils clean and use a sharp knife for cutting. The method for roasting peppers shown opposite is the easiest and quickest; if you prefer, you can roast peppers in a moderately hot oven for about 40 minutes, until blackened, then prepare as shown.

CUTTING VEGETABLES

MAKING JULIENNE STRIPS

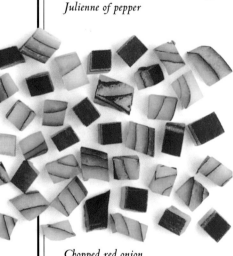

Julienne of pepper

1 Cut each pepper into quarters, then cut out the stem, core, and seeds.

2 Slice along the inside of the pepper pieces to remove the white membrane.

3 Hold the pepper pieces skin-side down and slice in long, narrow strips.

CHOPPING AN ONION

Chopped red onion

1 Peel the onion and trim the top. Cut in half, then slice horizontally, leaving the root intact to hold the slices together.

2 Keep the onion cut-side down on a board, and slice through it, this time vertically, up to, but not through, the root.

3 Slice the onion vertically again, making the cuts at right angles to the first set, so that the onion falls away in dice.

SHREDDING CABBAGE

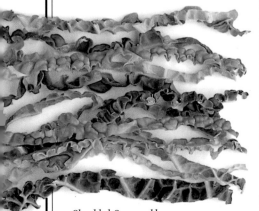

Shredded Savoy cabbage

1 Remove the outer leaves and, starting at the narrowest point, roll up each one tightly into a cigar shape.

2 Lay each rolled-up leaf on a work surface and cut across the roll to produce fine shreds of leaf.

3 Cut the remaining cabbage into quarters, cut the core out of each quarter, and slice across the leaves in fine shreds.

CUTTING HERBS

CHOPPING HERBS
Place the herbs on a chopping board. Rock a chef's knife up and down a few times across the leaves to chop them. Delicate herbs, such as basil, should be rolled and shredded in the same way as cabbage leaves (see left).

SNIPPING HERBS & PREPARING FRESH THYME
Hold a bunch of herbs over a bowl and snip into pieces with kitchen scissors, or place the herbs in a bowl and snip with the scissors. Strip the thyme leaves from the stalk before use.

MAKING A BOUQUET GARNI
A bouquet garni can be made with any herbs, and vegetables can also be added. This one was made by tying together thyme sprigs, a bay leaf, and celery stalks with a piece of plain string.

PREPARING & CHOPPING VEGETABLES

ROASTING PEPPERS

1 Cook the peppers whole under a preheated broiler for 10–12 minutes, until blackened.

2 Transfer to a plastic bag, seal, and cool. Remove the peppers and peel off the skins.

3 Pull out the cores, cut each pepper in half, and scrape out the seeds.

Roasted red pepper strips

CHOPPING GINGER

1 Carefully peel the ginger with a paring knife, then cut it into very thin slices, cutting across the grain.

2 Crush the ginger under the flat side of a chef's knife. Place in a pile and cut across the ginger to chop it finely.

CHOPPING GARLIC

Crush the garlic clove under the flat side of a chef's knife, then peel it. Use the knife to chop the crushed garlic finely.

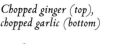

Chopped ginger (top), chopped garlic (bottom)

SKINNING, SEEDING & CHOPPING TOMATOES

1 Score crosses on the tops of the tomatoes. Place them in a pot of boiling water, leave for 30 seconds, then remove.

2 Pick up the split edges of the skin between your thumb and the blade of a sharp knife and peel off the skin.

3 Cut the tomatoes in half and squeeze out all the seeds with your hands. Finely chop the tomato halves.

Skinned and seeded tomato

COOKING METHODS

THE BASIC COOKING METHODS used in the recipes are explained in detail here, so use these pages as a reference guide in conjunction with the recipe section. The basic rules of each cooking method apply to whatever you are cooking. Follow them carefully to maximize the taste and preserve the natural goodness of ingredients. Roasting and broiling foods help seal in flavor; stir-frying retains the texture and nutrients; and sautéeing and braising moisten and add flavor to foods.

BASIC TECHNIQUES

STIR-FRYING

1 Assemble and prepare all the ingredients before you begin. Chop the ingredients into small, even-size pieces, so that they cook quickly and evenly.

2 Heat a little oil in a wok and, when hot, add the ingredients one by one, according to the recipe, or

beginning with those that will take longest to cook, such as onions and root vegetables.

3 Toss each ingredient vigorously for 1–2 minutes before adding the next. Do not fill the wok more than one third full, to ensure that all the ingredients cook properly.

Crunchy stir-fried vegetables retain plenty of nutrients and taste

SAUTEEING

Heat a little oil in a high-sided frying pan and cook ingredients over medium to high heat, stirring, until golden.

BRAISING

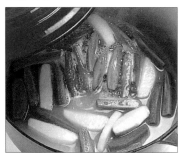

Carrots, celery, and other root vegetables are ideal for braising. Use a heavy skillet with a lid or a casserole. Put the prepared ingredients in the pan or casserole with enough stock, water, or wine to cover them. Bring to a boil, cover the pan tightly, and simmer over low heat until the ingredients are just tender.

TOASTING SPICES

Toasting spices brings out their taste and aroma. A wok is ideal for this purpose, but if you do not have one, use a frying pan or any other pan with a heavy bottom. Toss the spices vigorously over high heat, in a dry pan, for 2–3 minutes, until their aroma is released. Use as directed.

COOKING DRIED LEGUMES

All dried legumes, except lentils, need to be soaked overnight in water. After they have soaked, drain and rinse them, and place in a pot with twice their own volume of water. Always boil dried peas and beans rapidly for 10 minutes, then drain. Place in fresh water, bring to a boil, then simmer for the time shown.

COOKING TIMES FOR DRIED LEGUMES

Adzuki beans	45 minutes	Haricot beans	1–1½ hours
Black beans	1–1½ hours	Lentils	20–30 minutes
Black-eyed beans	1–1½ hours	Lima beans	1–1½ hours
Borlotti beans	1–1½ hours	Mung beans	1 hour
Cannellini beans	1–1½ hours	Pinto beans	1–1½ hours
Chickpeas	2 hours	Red kidney beans	1¾ hours
Flageolet beans	1–1½ hours	Soybeans	3½–4 hours
Great Northern beans	2½–4 hours	Split peas	2 hours

DEEP-FRYING

1 Fill a deep-fat fryer one third full with oil. Heat the oil until hot. Drop a cube of bread into the fat. If it browns immediately, the oil is hot enough.

2 Fry the food in batches to prevent overcrowding. Cook according to the recipe. Drain on paper towels.

ROASTING VEGETABLES

Prepare the vegetables and cut them into large, even-size chunks. Place in a roasting pan and drizzle with olive oil. Roast in a preheated oven at 450°F/230°C for 40 minutes, until golden and tender. Whole bulbs of garlic halved and roasted in this way have a delicious, sweet flavor.

BROILING VEGETABLES

Prepare and trim the vegetables to be broiled, then halve them or cut them into thick slices. Brush them lightly with olive oil and broil under a hot, preheated broiler, turning them at least once, until tender all the way through and slightly charred on all sides.

GRILLING VEGETABLES

Heat a ridged grill pan over high heat. Prepare the vegetables the same way as for broiling and place them on the hot pan. Cook the vegetables over high heat, turning them at least once, until tender and slightly charred on both sides.

Cooking vegetables on a ridged grill pan creates attractive, charred stripes

PASTRY

ALTHOUGH FRESH PASTRY is now available in most supermarkets, preparing your own is well worth the effort. The key to good pastry is to work in a cool kitchen with cold ingredients and cold hands, and to handle the pastry as little as possible. All pastry doughs are enriched with fat. Some contain eggs, milk, or sugar, and can be flavored according to taste with nuts, dried fruit, spices, herbs, or cheese. If you do not have time to make your own pastry, be sure to buy a brand that does not contain animal fat.

SHORT CRUST PASTRY
Makes enough for 2 shells or 1 double crust

Short crust is the simplest pastry to make and can be used for most tarts and pies. Unless the recipe states otherwise, it is best cooked in a metal pan and baked blind before filling (see below, right), which keeps it crisp.

2 cups (250g) all-purpose flour, sifted, plus extra, to dust
¾ cup (175g) chilled, unsalted butter, cubed
1 egg, beaten
pinch of salt

1 Place the flour in a bowl and add the butter. Rub the butter into the flour with your fingertips until the mixture resembles fine bread crumbs.

2 Make a well in the center and pour in the beaten egg. Add the pinch of salt.

3 Gently mix together with your fingertips to form a smooth dough.

4 Bring the dough together into a rough ball and wrap it in plastic wrap. Let rest in the refrigerator for 30 minutes before use.

Plastic wrap keeps dough moist

SWEET PASTRY
Makes enough for 2 shells or 1 double crust

This pastry is ideal for making sweet tarts and pies.

2⅔ cups (325g) all-purpose flour, sifted, plus extra, to dust
1 cup (225g) unsalted butter, at room temperature, cut in small pieces
pinch of salt
1 cup (200g) confectioners' sugar, sifted
finely grated zest of ½ lemon
1 egg, beaten

1 Place the flour in a bowl and make a well in the center. Add the butter, salt, sugar, lemon zest, and egg.

2 Gradually mix in the flour with your fingertips until the ingredients come together to form a soft dough. Knead for 1 minute until smooth. Form into a ball, cover, and chill for 2 hours before use.

BAKING BLIND

1 Roll out the pastry and use the rolling pin to lift and transfer it into the pan.

2 Prick the pastry with a fork to prevent it from rising up during baking.

3 Line the pastry shell with waxed paper and fill with baking beans before cooking according to the recipe.

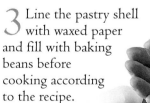

You can use ceramic or dried beans or rice

PASTA

MAKING FRESH PASTA is easy. The dough can be mixed by hand on a clean work surface or made in a food processor. To use a food processor, put in the flour, salt, and olive oil, add the beaten eggs and egg yolk, and process until the mixture forms a dough. This takes a few seconds — it is important not to overwork the dough. Remove the dough from the food processor. If it is too dry, add a little water and knead in. If it is too wet, sprinkle with flour. Knead well, then cover, and let rest.

— MAKING THE DOUGH —

Makes 13oz (375g)

It is best to handle this amount of ingredients on a clean work surface, but if you want to make half the quantity of dough, it may be easier to mix it in a bowl.

2¼ cups (250g) all-purpose flour, plus extra, to dust
pinch of salt
2 large eggs, plus 1 large egg yolk
1 tbsp extra virgin olive oil
1 tbsp water

1 Sift the flour and salt onto a clean work surface, and form it into a mound. Make a well in the center of the flour with your fingertips.

2 Put the eggs and egg yolk into the well in the flour, then add the oil and water. Gradually bring the flour into the center with your fingertips.

3 Mix the flour into the eggs with your fingers until the ingredients are combined into a smooth paste. Gather the dough into a rough ball.

4 Knead the dough for 4–5 minutes, until smooth and elastic. Cover in plastic wrap and let rest for 30 minutes before rolling it out.

Knead dough with heel of your hand

— ROLLING & CUTTING —

A small, hand-operated pasta machine is the best tool for rolling out pasta dough. Not only does it roll out pasta accurately to the desired thickness but it also helps knead the dough. Pasta machines vary in size and price, but a basic model will do the job adequately. You will need to buy various cutting attachments to cut different shapes. If the dough sticks, dust it with a little flour.

1 Divide the dough into four. Sprinkle with flour on all sides, put the machine on the widest setting, then feed a piece of dough through the rollers.

2 Change the setting on the machine by one notch. Fold the pasta in half, dust with flour, then feed it through the rollers once again.

3 Repeat the process four or five times, decreasing the space between the rollers each time, until the pasta reaches the desired thickness.

4 Lay the pasta sheets on dish towels to dry for 5–10 minutes. Attach the appropriate cutter to the machine and feed the pasta through. For lasagna and cannelloni, cut by hand.

Guide pasta sheet through rollers with your hand

BASIC RECIPES

STOCKS ARE NOT as time-consuming to make as is often believed. Simply let the stock bubble away while you prepare the recipe. The recipes in this book call for specific stocks. Some recipes require a delicately flavored vegetable stock, while others require the deeper flavor of a mushroom stock. Always use fresh, good quality ingredients for the most nutritious and flavorful results.

STOCKS & SAUCES

VEGETABLE STOCK

Makes 4½ cups (1 liter)

2 tbsp extra virgin olive oil

1 onion, roughly chopped

1 small leek, roughly chopped

¾ cup (75g) celeriac, roughly chopped

2 large carrots, roughly chopped

1 celery stalk, roughly chopped

¾ cup (75g) white cabbage, roughly chopped

½ fennel, roughly chopped

4 garlic cloves, chopped

½ cup (125ml) white wine, optional

4 black peppercorns

1 thyme sprig

1 small bay leaf

2 tsp sea salt

1 Heat the olive oil in a large pan, add all the vegetables and garlic, and cook over low heat for about 5 minutes.

2 Pour in the wine, if using, then add the peppercorns, thyme, bay leaf, and 6¼ cups (1.4 liters) water. Bring to a boil, add the sea salt, and skim off any scum. Reduce the heat to very low and simmer the stock gently for 40 minutes, until reduced by one third of its original volume.

3 Strain the stock through a fine sieve and let cool. Cover and keep in the refrigerator until needed, but for a maximum of 1 week.

DARK VEGETABLE STOCK

Makes 4½ cups (1 liter)

4 tbsp vegetable oil

½ onion, roughly chopped

2 large carrots, roughly chopped

1 leek, roughly chopped

1 celery stalk, roughly chopped

2 garlic cloves, chopped

¼lb (100g) mushrooms, roughly chopped

2 ripe beefsteak tomatoes, roughly chopped

2 thyme sprigs

a few parsley sprigs

1 bay leaf

1 heaping tsp granulated sugar

½ tbsp sea salt

2 tbsp dark soy sauce

1 Heat the vegetable oil in a large pan, add the onion, carrots, leek, celery, and garlic, and sauté over medium heat for about 5 minutes, until lightly colored.

2 Add the mushrooms and sauté for 5 minutes over low heat until golden. Add the tomatoes, herbs, and sugar and cook for 5 minutes longer. Stir in 6¼ cups (1.4 liters) water. Bring to a boil, add sea salt, and skim off any scum. Simmer the stock gently for 45 minutes.

3 Stir in the soy sauce, strain through a fine sieve, and cool. Cover and keep in the refrigerator (see left).

BROWN MUSHROOM STOCK

Makes 4½ cups (1 liter)

7 tbsp (100g) unsalted butter

3 shallots, finely diced

2 garlic cloves, sliced

1¾lb (800g) mushrooms, roughly chopped

1 tbsp tomato paste

4 medium ripe tomatoes, roughly chopped

a few parsley sprigs

4 tbsp tamari

1 Melt the butter, add the shallots and garlic, and sweat them over medium heat until softened.

2 Add the mushrooms and cook, stirring, until they are deep brown and lightly caramelized. Stir in the tomato paste and tomatoes and simmer for 10 minutes.

3 Pour in 7½ cups (1.7 liters) water, add the parsley, and bring to a boil. Skim any scum off the surface of the stock with a slotted spoon, then reduce the heat and simmer for 25 minutes. Stir in the tamari and remove from the heat.

4 Strain the stock through a fine sieve and let it completely cool. Cover and keep in the refrigerator until required (see left).

MADEIRA SAUCE

Makes 2½ cups (600ml)

4 tbsp vegetable oil

½ onion, roughly chopped

2 large carrots, chopped

1 leek, chopped

1 celery stalk, chopped

2 garlic cloves, chopped

¼lb (100g) mushrooms, chopped

2 large tomatoes, chopped

2 thyme sprigs

1 bay leaf

1 tsp superfine sugar

1 tsp salt

2 tbsp (25g) unsalted butter

1oz (25g) porcini, soaked in water, drained, and chopped

2 tbsp Madeira

1 Heat the oil, add the onion, carrots, leek, celery, and garlic, and sauté over medium heat for 5 minutes. Add the mushrooms and cook for 5 minutes longer.

2 Stir in the tomatoes, herbs, and sugar and simmer gently for 5 minutes. Add 3¾ cups (850ml) water, bring to a boil, then add the salt. Simmer for 45 minutes. Strain through a fine sieve.

3 Heat the butter and cook the porcini for 2 minutes over low heat. Pour in the Madeira and stock. Simmer until reduced by half. Season.

OTHER USEFUL RECIPES

ROASTED CHERRY TOMATO SALSA

Serves 4

½ lb (250g) cherry tomatoes, halved

1 garlic clove, crushed

1 tbsp chopped fresh basil

good pinch of superfine sugar

4 tbsp olive oil

2 tbsp lime or lemon juice

salt and freshly ground pepper

Preheat the oven to 475°F/240°C. Place the cherry tomatoes and garlic in a roasting pan. Sprinkle with the basil and sugar, then drizzle with 2 tablespoons of olive oil. Season, then bake for 2–3 minutes, until the tomatoes are just tender. Transfer the tomatoes to a large bowl. Add the lime juice and remaining olive oil and toss together gently to mix. Serve warm or cold.

FRESH TOMATO SAUCE

Makes 1¼ cups (300ml)

6 tbsp olive oil

½ onion, roughly chopped

2 garlic cloves, crushed

fresh thyme sprig

1½ lb (750g) ripe tomatoes

1 tbsp tomato paste

pinch of superfine sugar

salt and freshly ground pepper

1¾ cups (425ml) Vegetable Stock (see opposite)

Heat the olive oil in a pan, add the onion, garlic, and thyme, and sweat over medium heat until soft. Roughly chop the tomatoes and add to the pan with the tomato paste and sugar. Season, then add the vegetable stock. Bring to a boil. Reduce the heat and simmer for 10–15 minutes, until the tomatoes are reduced to a pulp. Strain the sauce through a fine sieve to serve.

LEMON PEPPER

Preheat the oven to 325°F/160°C. Peel 4 lemons with a potato peeler. Spread the peel out on a clean baking sheet and bake for 1 hour, until the skins are dried and shriveled. Let cool. When cool, place the peel in a coffee grinder, in small batches, and grind to a fine powder. Store the lemon pepper in an airtight container for up to 1 month.

VINAIGRETTE

Makes about ¾ cup (200ml)

3 tbsp quality red wine vinegar

1–1½ tbsp Dijon mustard

1 small garlic clove, crushed

5 tbsp extra virgin olive oil

5 tbsp peanut or vegetable oil

salt and freshly ground pepper

Mix the vinegar, mustard, and garlic in a bowl. Pour in the oils and whisk. Season.

OLIVADA

Makes ¾ cup (150g)

1 cup (125g) pitted black olives, finely chopped

2 garlic cloves

4 tbsp olive oil

salt and freshly ground pepper

Blend all the ingredients to a coarse puree in a blender or food processor. Transfer to a bowl, cover, and store in the refrigerator for up to 4 days.

LABNA

Line a colander with four layers of dampened cheesecloth. Pour 1 cup (250g) yogurt into the cloth, gather together the edges, tie them, and suspend over a bowl. Let drain in a cool place for 3–4 days, or a minimum of 1 day. When the milky liquid has drained off, it will leave about ½ cup (125g) of thick, creamy yogurt. This amount will serve four.

RECIPES

THIS COLLECTION OF RECIPES WILL CHANGE THE WAY YOU

THINK ABOUT VEGETARIAN COOKING. THE DISHES

MAKE USE OF THE ARRAY OF PRODUCE AND FLAVORINGS THAT IS

AVAILABLE TO US FROM AROUND THE WORLD,

TO PRODUCE A NEW GENERATION OF VEGETARIAN CUISINE.

CLASSIC RECIPES ARE GIVEN NEW INTERPRETATIONS,

AND NOVEL AND EXCITING COMBINATIONS OF INGREDIENTS

ARE USED FOR MAXIMUM IMPACT.

APPETIZERS & FINGER FOOD

THESE RECIPES DRAW ON influences from every corner of the globe, including South America, the Mediterranean, the Middle East, and Asia. Their wonderful flavors and textures range from simple and rustic to elegant and refined: there is something suitable for every occasion. Although the recipes in this chapter are specifically designed to whet the appetite, and will provide an impressive prelude to any meal, they also make delicious light meals suitable for serving as main courses.

—— LAYERED MEDITERRANEAN GATEAU WITH LABNA ——

KEY INGREDIENTS

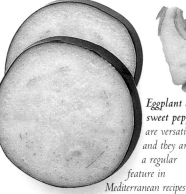

Basil is highly aromatic and gives a wonderful flavor to many Mediterranean dishes

Labna is an easy-to-make strained yogurt

Eggplant and sweet peppers are versatile and they are a regular feature in Mediterranean recipes

Cilantro is useful as a garnish or in cooking

Tomatoes are delicious served simply

Our passion for the light, fresh, healthy cooking of the Mediterranean continues to grow and grow. This layered savory gâteau is not only visually stunning but also bursting with flavor. Labna is a strained yogurt that is easy to make and well worth the effort. If you do not have a ring mold just carefully build the layers of vegetables on the baking sheet.

INGREDIENTS

1 cup (200ml) olive oil, plus oil, to grease

1 eggplant, cut into ¼ inch (5mm) slices

handful of fresh basil leaves

1 garlic clove

4 peppers (2 red, 1 yellow, 1 green) roasted, peeled, seeded (see page 39), and quartered

4 plum tomatoes, cut into thick slices

4 tbsp Labna (see page 45)

fresh basil sprig, to garnish

FOR THE VINAIGRETTE

2 tbsp chopped fresh basil or cilantro

2 tbsp red wine vinegar

6 tbsp olive oil

1 tomato, peeled, seeded, and chopped (see page 39)

salt and freshly ground pepper

1 Heat ⅔ cup (150ml) of the olive oil in a heavy-bottomed skillet. Cook the eggplant for 5 minutes on each side over medium heat until golden. Drain.

2 In a blender or food processor, puree together the basil and garlic with 2 tablespoons of olive oil. Place four 3 inch (7cm) metal ring molds on a lightly greased baking sheet.

3 Layer the vegetables in the molds: start with a slice of eggplant, then continue with 1 teaspoon of basil puree, alternate pieces of the red, yellow, and green pepper, more basil puree, another slice of eggplant, then basil puree again. Top with a layer of tomatoes.

4 Press down lightly, drizzle with the remaining olive oil, then bake for 10 minutes. Place the molds on serving plates, then carefully lift off the molds. Blend together all the ingredients for the vinaigrette. To serve, garnish each gâteau with a spoonful of labna, a drizzle of vinaigrette, and a sprig of basil.

Oven preheated to 350°F/180°C

Preparation & cooking time 50 minutes

Serves 4

Nutritional notes calories 693; protein 5g; carbohydrates 14g; total fat 69g, of which saturated fat 10g; fiber 4g; sodium 145mg

GOAT CHEESE LATKES WITH BEET SALSA

This sumptuous version of the famous Jewish potato pancake includes zucchini, which provide both color and flavor, and a rich, tangy goat cheese filling. The salsa is a modern interpretation of classical Eastern European flavors.

INGREDIENTS

1 lb (450g) starchy potatoes, peeled
1 medium zucchini
1 large onion
4 goat cheeses, about 3oz (75g) each
salt and freshly ground pepper
1 egg yolk, beaten
3 tbsp arrowroot or potato flour
vegetable oil, for frying
sour cream, to serve
fresh basil leaves, to garnish

FOR THE SALSA

2 medium beets, boiled and diced
2 shallots, chopped
¼ tsp caraway seeds
2 tbsp red wine vinegar
2 tbsp olive oil
2 tbsp chopped fresh basil
1 red chili, seeded and chopped
1 tbsp maple syrup or honey

1 For the salsa, place the diced beets in a bowl and add the remaining ingredients. Season, then stir to combine. Cover and marinate for about 2 hours.

2 Grate the potatoes, zucchini, and onion on the largest holes of the grater, then put them in a clean dish towel and squeeze out any excess moisture. Transfer to a bowl, season, and stir in the egg yolk until thoroughly mixed. Sift in the arrowroot and beat vigorously until well combined.

3 Heat the oil in a frying pan. Dip the cheeses in the batter to coat them, then place, well spaced out, in the pan. Cook over medium heat for 2–3 minutes on each side until golden, then drain on paper towels. Serve with sour cream and an ample spoonful of salsa, and garnish with basil leaves.

Preparation & cooking time
1 hour, plus 2 hours marinating time

Serves 4

Nutritional notes
calories 684; protein 27g; carbohydrates 55g; total fat 41g, of which saturated fat 21g; fiber 3g; sodium 645mg

---

CAPONATA ON ROASTED GARLIC BRUSCHETTA

Caponata, a sweet-and-sour stew from Sicily, makes a wonderful topping for bruschetta. Roasting the garlic gives a mellow sweetness that contrasts well with the piquancy of the vegetables.

INGREDIENTS

½ medium eggplant
3 peppers (1 red, 1 yellow, 1 green), seeded
1 zucchini
2 celery sticks
1 red onion, sliced
2 tbsp honey
2 tbsp balsamic vinegar
1 tbsp raisins, soaked overnight in water
1 tbsp pine nuts, toasted
salt and freshly ground pepper

FOR THE BRUSCHETTA

3 whole garlic cloves, unpeeled
5 tbsp olive oil
8 thick slices Italian bread
thin shavings Parmesan
basil and arugula leaves, to garnish

1 In a small, ovenproof dish, toss the garlic in 1 tablespoon of olive oil and roast for 30 minutes, until soft and caramelized; set aside.

2 Cut the vegetables into ½ inch (1cm) pieces. In a pan, heat 2 tablespoons of olive oil and sauté the onion for 5 minutes over medium heat, until golden. Add the remaining vegetables and cook over low heat for about 10 minutes until tender. Stir in the remaining ingredients; season.

3 Brush the bread slices with the remaining oil and bake for 10 minutes, until golden. Squeeze the roasted garlic out of its skin and spread over the toast, then pile on the vegetables. Top with Parmesan, basil, and arugula.

Oven preheated to
400°F/200°C

Preparation & cooking time
1 hour, plus overnight soaking time

Serves 4

Nutritional notes
calories 557; protein 16g; carbohydrates 81g; total fat 21g, of which saturated fat 3g; fiber 9g; sodium 1708mg

GRILLED ASPARAGUS WITH TOPPING

Asparagus are usually served steamed, but I find that they have a much better flavor when grilled because the direct contact with the heat caramelizes them slightly. Choose very fresh, brightly colored stems — if they are at all withered they will be tough and bitter.

INGREDIENTS

finely grated zest of 1 lemon

2 tbsp chopped fresh flat-leaf parsley

1 tbsp chopped fresh basil

⅔ cup (150ml) Vinaigrette (see page 45)

32 fat asparagus stalks, trimmed

6 tbsp olive oil

salt and freshly ground pepper

FOR THE TOPPING

3 slices white bread, crusts removed

3 tbsp (50g) butter, melted

1 For the topping, process the bread to a coarse, crumblike texture in a blender or food processor, then mix in the butter. Spread on a baking sheet, then bake for 15 minutes until golden.

2 Meanwhile, stir the lemon zest and chopped herbs into the vinaigrette. Put the asparagus on wooden skewers that have been soaked in water (about six per skewer), so that they lie across the skewers (this makes it easier to turn them). Place in a dish, pour the olive oil over them, season, and let sit for 5–10 minutes to allow the salt to tenderize them slightly.

3 Grill the asparagus on a heated grill pan or under a hot broiler for 4 minutes until tender, turning them occasionally.

4 To serve, remove the skewers and place the asparagus on a large serving plate. Drizzle with the vinaigrette, then scatter the topping over the top.

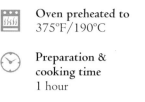

Oven preheated to
375°F/190°C

Preparation & cooking time
1 hour

Serves 4

Nutritional notes
calories 480; protein 9g; carbohydrates 16g; total fat 43g, of which saturated fat 11g; fiber 4g; sodium 295mg

---

SAVORY ROQUEFORT MOUSSE

This delicious mousse is simple and quick to make. The sauce can be prepared in advance, one or two hours before needed, but do not put it in the refrigerator, because this will spoil the texture.

INGREDIENTS

1¼ cups (300ml) milk

3 tbsp (50g) unsalted butter, plus extra, to grease

⅓ cup (50g) all-purpose flour

3 eggs, plus 2 egg yolks

1 cup (250ml) light cream

2oz (50g) cream cheese

¼lb (75g) Roquefort, mashed

salt and freshly ground pepper

pinch ground nutmeg

FOR THE ROASTED PEPPER SAUCE

2 large red peppers, roasted, peeled, seeded (see page 39), and chopped

1¼ cups (300ml) Vegetable Stock (see page 44)

2 tbsp olive oil

1 For the roasted pepper sauce, place the peppers in a blender or food processor with the stock, olive oil, and seasoning. Blend to a smooth paste.

2 In a small pan, bring the milk and butter to a boil. Sift in the flour and beat well until the mixture thickens. Reduce the heat to low and continue to cook for 2 minutes, beating continuously.

3 Add the eggs, egg yolks, and cream to the pan, beating to form a thick sauce. Stir in the cream cheese, Roquefort, salt, pepper, and nutmeg.

4 Butter four individual ramekins and fill with the cheese mixture. Place the ramekins in a roasting pan, then pour in enough boiling water to come one third of the way up the sides.

5 Bake for 15–20 minutes, until lightly set and golden. Turn the mousses out onto serving plates. To serve, heat the roasted pepper sauce and pour a little sauce around each mousse.

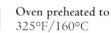

Oven preheated to
325°F/160°C

Preparation & cooking time
1¼ hours, plus 1 hour for the stock

Serves 4

Nutritional notes
calories 392; protein 14g; carbohydrates 10g; total fat 33g, of which saturated fat 16g; fiber 2g; sodium 527mg

WOK & ROLL

These delightful, tiny spring rolls have a classic elegance that I associate with Chinese cuisine. They are light and crispy on the outside and moist and delicately spicy on the inside. Ready-to-use spring roll wrappers are now more widely available in supermarkets than they were in the past. The beauty of these spring rolls is that they can be prepared in advance up to the end of step three and frozen for up to three months. Serve with Chinese Dipping Sauce (see below).

INGREDIENTS

12 spring roll wrappers,
each about 8 inches (20cm) square

1 egg, beaten

vegetable oil, for deep-frying

1 tbsp black or toasted sesame seeds

Chinese Dipping Sauce (see below), to serve

FOR THE STIR-FRY

4 tbsp vegetable oil

1 garlic clove, crushed

1½ inch (4cm) piece of fresh
ginger, chopped

½ green pepper, cored, seeded,
and cut in julienne strips

1 celery stalk, thinly sliced

1 carrot, cut in julienne strips

½ cup (50g) Chinese cabbage, shredded

2 tbsp hoisin sauce

salt and freshly ground pepper

FOR THE SLAW

¼ cucumber, shredded

½ cup (50g) bean sprouts

1 small red chili, seeded and thinly sliced

4 tbsp rice wine vinegar

4 tbsp light soy sauce

2 tbsp maple syrup

1 For the stir-fry, heat a wok over high heat until it is very hot, then add the oil. Cook the garlic and ginger for a few seconds to flavor the oil, then stir-fry the vegetables. Add the green pepper first and stir-fry for 1 minute, then add the celery and stir-fry for a minute. Next add the carrot and Chinese cabbage. Continue cooking for 1 minute more, then season. Place in a bowl to cool, then refrigerate.

2 For the slaw, put the shredded cucumber, bean sprouts, and red chili in a bowl. Blend together the rice wine vinegar, soy sauce, and maple syrup, then mix into the slaw. Cover and set aside. Mix the hoisin sauce in with the stir-fried vegetables; adjust the seasoning.

3 Lay the spring roll wrappers on a work surface and brush with beaten egg. Put 1 tablespoon of the stir-fry in the center of each wrapper, fold the edges in a little, then roll the wrapper up tightly into a cigar shape. Seal the edges with beaten egg.

4 Heat the oil in the wok. Deep-fry the rolls, a few at a time, for 3 minutes, until golden. Drain. Place a portion of slaw on each plate and lay two spring rolls on top. Scatter with the sesame seeds. Serve with dipping sauce.

Preparation & cooking time
40 minutes,
plus 1 hour for
the dipping sauce

Serves 4

Nutritional notes
calories 459; protein 9g;
carbohydrates 38g;
total fat 31g, of which
saturated fat 4g;
fiber 2g; sodium 1617mg

CHINESE DIPPING SAUCE

Dipping sauces form an integral part of Chinese cooking, and this sauce is one of my particular favorites. I often use it as a base for a salad dressing, add it to stir-fries, or serve it with Wok & Roll (see above).

INGREDIENTS

1 tbsp light soy sauce

2 shallots, finely chopped

2 tbsp rice wine vinegar

2 tsp sesame oil

½ tbsp superfine sugar

½ inch (1cm) piece of fresh ginger,
finely grated

½ small red chili, seeded and
finely chopped

Mix together all the sauce ingredients in a bowl and stir until well combined. Cover and chill in the refrigerator, to allow the flavors to infuse, for at least 1 hour before serving. Serves four.

GRECQUE OF VEGETABLES WITH HERB CHEESE

Although this recipe is not an authentically Greek one, it captures some typical flavors and textures. The herb cheese is simple to make and versatile; it spreads well for sandwiches and makes a wonderful dip. Basil, parsley, and tarragon make a good herb mix for flavoring the cheese. Chanterelles are best for this recipe, but if they are not available, you can replace them with commercial mushrooms. Serve the dish with warm pita bread.

INGREDIENTS

6 tbsp olive oil

½lb (250g) baby zucchini, halved lengthwise

12 scallions, trimmed

½lb (250g) chanterelles

1 garlic clove, crushed

juice of 2 lemons

1 tsp coriander seeds

1 bay leaf

leaves from sprig of fresh thyme

⅔ cup (150ml) dry white wine

lightly cracked black peppercorns

chives, to garnish

FOR THE HERB CHEESE

5½oz (150g) feta

3½oz (100g) cream cheese

1 garlic clove, crushed

1 tbsp chopped mixed fresh herbs

4 tbsp heavy cream

pinch cayenne pepper

salt and freshly ground pepper

1 Heat the oil in a skillet. Sauté the zucchini, onions, and chanterelles over medium to high heat for 2–3 minutes. Reduce the heat to medium and add the remaining ingredients. Cook, stirring, for a further 8–10 minutes. When the vegetables are just tender, but not too soft, remove from the heat and let cool.

2 For the herb cheese, blend together the feta, cream cheese, and garlic in a blender or food processor. Add the mixed herbs, then blend again. Stir in the cream and cayenne pepper, and season. Form the herb cheese into eight oval quenelles, using two dessert spoons.

3 Divide the vegetables among four plates. Place two herb cheese quenelles on each plate and garnish with chives, then serve.

 Preparation & cooking time
50 minutes

Serves 4

Nutritional notes
calories 534; protein 10g;
carbohydrates 4g;
total fat 51g, of which
saturated fat 24g;
fiber 1g; sodium 733mg

STACKED VEGETABLE CEVICHE

Ceviche is a South American dish of thinly sliced raw fish "cooked" in a chili-spiced, citrus marinade. I have used the same flavorings in this dressing for crunchy raw vegetables, layered between crispy corn tortillas, for a very special appetizer.

INGREDIENTS

1 medium cauliflower, cut into small florets

2 tomatoes, peeled, seeded, and chopped (see page 39)

1 small cucumber, peeled and diced

1 small green apple, peeled and diced

2 smooth-skinned avocados, diced and sprinkled with lemon juice

4 radicchio, shredded

4 scallions, shredded

8 corn tortillas, deep-fried until crisp

mizuna leaves, to garnish

FOR THE DRESSING

1 red chili

juice of 2 limes

zest and juice of 1 orange

1 tbsp coriander seeds, crushed

½ tsp superfine sugar

1 garlic clove, crushed

2 tbsp sour cream

2 tbsp chopped fresh cilantro

1 For the dressing, roast the chili for 15 minutes, then, when cool enough to handle, cut in half, remove the seeds, and chop the chili finely. Place in a bowl and toss together with the remaining ingredients. Cover, and set aside to marinate for about 4 hours.

2 Blanch the cauliflower florets in boiling, salted water for 2 minutes. Refresh in cold water, drain, and place in a clean bowl. Add the tomatoes, cucumber, apple, avocados, radicchio, and scallions.

3 Pour the dressing over the vegetables. Cover with plastic wrap and let marinate in the refrigerator for a further 30 minutes. Serve chilled, layering the vegetables between the crispy fried tortillas (serving two tortillas per person). Garnish each one with a cilantro leaf.

Oven preheated to 425°F/220°C

Preparation & cooking time 30 minutes, plus 4 hours marinating time

Serves 4

Nutritional notes calories 402; protein 14g; carbohydrates 80g; total fat 6g, of which saturated fat 2g; fiber 7g; sodium 333mg

MINTED ASPARAGUS TARTLETS

Filled with a puree of asparagus and fromage frais, these tartlets are deliciously light. I love the combination of asparagus and mint — perfect for an early summer meal. Alternatively, you could use other herbs, such as basil, parsley, or chervil.

INGREDIENTS

1 batch Short Crust Pastry (see page 42)

1lb (400g) asparagus, trimmed

3½oz (100g) fromage frais

2 tbsp (25g) butter, plus extra, to grease

1 onion, chopped

1 garlic clove, crushed

2 tbsp chopped fresh mint

¼ cup (25g) all-purpose flour

salt and freshly ground pepper

1 Grease four 3 inch (7cm) tart pans. Roll out the pastry on a floured surface and use to line the tart pans. Cover with waxed paper and baking beans, and bake blind for 5–6 minutes. Remove the paper and beans, and bake for a further 3–4 minutes; let cool.

2 Steam the asparagus for 2–3 minutes, until just tender. Drain and refresh in cold water. Trim the tips and reserve them. Place the stems in a blender or food processor with the fromage frais; blend until smooth.

3 Melt the butter in a small pan, add the onion, garlic, and mint, and sauté over low heat for 2 minutes until softened. Sift in the flour, stir well, and cook for a further 2 minutes. Stir in the asparagus puree, then whisk over low heat until the sauce is thick. Season to taste.

4 Pour the sauce into the pastry shells, arrange the asparagus tips on top, and bake for 5 minutes longer. Serve hot or cold.

Oven preheated to 375°F/190°C

Preparation & cooking time 35 minutes, plus 40 minutes for the pastry

Serves 4

Nutritional notes calories 418; protein 10g; carbohydrate 36g; total fat 27g, of which saturated fat 17g; fiber 3g; sodium 123mg

BLACK BEAN FALAFEL

Falafel is virtually Israel's national dish. These little chickpea fritters are usually eaten stuffed into warm pita bread and served with a tahini dressing. Here they are presented elegantly on a bed of salad with baked red onions and crisp spinach (see Red Onion Salad with Tahini Dressing, below).

INGREDIENTS

4 slices white bread, crusts removed

1lb (450g) chickpeas, soaked in cold water for 24 hours

¼ cup (25g) all-purpose or chickpea flour

1 medium onion, roughly chopped

2 tbsp chopped fresh parsley

2 tbsp chopped fresh cilantro

2 large garlic cloves, crushed

1 tsp cayenne pepper

1 tsp ground cumin

1 cup (200g) dried black beans, soaked overnight, cooked (see page 41), and drained

vegetable oil, for frying

Red Onion Salad with Tahini Dressing (see below), to serve

1 Place the bread in a bowl. Pour ⅔ cup (150ml) of cold water over the bread. Let soak for 10 minutes.

2 Drain the chickpeas and chop to a fine pulp in a blender or food processor. Transfer to a bowl with the flour.

3 Mince the onion, parsley, and cilantro in a blender or food processor, then add the garlic, cayenne pepper, and cumin. Blend again, then mix with the chickpeas and flour.

4 Squeeze the excess water from the bread with your hands and add to the mixture. Work all the ingredients together until well blended, then stir in the cooked black beans and mix until thoroughly incorporated.

5 Shape into small cakes, approximately 2 inches (5cm) in diameter and ¾ inch (2cm) thick. Let rest in the refrigerator for 30 minutes, until the mixture has firmed up.

6 Heat the oil in a large skillet and shallow-fry the falafel for 3–4 minutes on each side over medium heat until golden. Drain the excess oil on paper towels. Serve on a bed of the red onion salad with tahini dressing.

Preparation & cooking time
2½ hours, plus 24 hours soaking time

Serves 4

Nutritional notes
calories 878; protein 26g; carbohydrates 68g; total fat 58g, of which saturated fat 8g; fiber 12g; sodium 438mg

RED ONION SALAD WITH TAHINI DRESSING

The inclusion of mustard in the tahini dressing is unusual, but it gives a nice bite. The onions have a wonderfully sweet and tangy flavor when mixed with the dressing and baked. Serve with the Black Bean Falafel (see above).

INGREDIENTS

FOR THE SALAD

2 red onions

¾lb (300g) young spinach

FOR THE TAHINI DRESSING

6 tbsp water

3 tbsp white wine vinegar

3 tbsp tahini

2 tbsp coarse-grain mustard

1 tbsp honey

1 garlic clove, crushed

½ cup (125ml) olive oil

1 For the dressing, whisk together all the ingredients in a bowl until smooth.

2 Peel the onions without removing the roots, then cut the onions into separate wedges (the root holds the wedges intact). Place in a baking dish and cover with half the dressing. Let marinate for 2 hours, then bake for 30 minutes, until tender.

3 Place the spinach in a bowl, add the onions, and the remaining dressing, reserving just a little to serve. Toss until the salad is well coated.

4 Divide the onion salad equally among four serving plates, and drizzle with the remaining dressing.

Oven preheated to 400°F/200°C

Preparation & cooking time
55 minutes, plus 2 hours marinating time

Serves 4

Nutritional notes
calories 455; protein 7g; carbohydrates 15g; total fat 41g, of which saturated fat 6g; fiber 5g; sodium 226mg

ASIAN MUSHROOM SUSHI PURSES

With a surprise filling of shiitake mushrooms spiced with searingly hot Japanese horseradish, these little pastry purses taste as good as they look. They can be assembled in advance and cooked just before serving. Serve with a bowl of soy or plum sauce for dipping.

INGREDIENTS

¾ cup (150g) short-grain rice
½ tsp granulated sugar
¼ cup (50ml) rice wine vinegar
2 tbsp sesame oil
1 garlic clove, crushed
3oz (75g) shiitake mushrooms, sliced
¼ tsp wasabi (Japanese horseradish)
2 scallions, shredded
1 tbsp soy sauce
20 spring roll or wonton wrappers
1 egg, beaten
1 tbsp black or toasted sesame seeds
vegetable oil, for deep-frying
salt and freshly ground pepper

1 Boil the rice for 20 minutes according to package instructions, until tender. Remove from the heat and let stand, covered, for 10 minutes.

2 Place the sugar and vinegar in a large pan and heat them together over low heat, stirring until the sugar has dissolved. Stir in the hot rice and let cool.

3 Heat the sesame oil and sauté the garlic and mushrooms over medium heat for 2–3 minutes. Place in a bowl with the wasabi, scallions, and soy sauce, then season.

4 To assemble, dampen your hands with water and roll the rice into 1 inch (2.5cm) balls. Make a small hole in the center of each rice ball with your thumb. Spoon a little of the mushroom and onion filling into the hole. Close up the rice around the filling. Repeat until all the mixture is used.

5 Lay the spring roll wrappers on a clean work surface and brush them liberally with the beaten egg. Place a rice ball on each wrapper, then draw up the corners of the wrapper to form a small purse. Push the neck together to seal in the rice ball.

6 Brush with beaten egg, then sprinkle with sesame seeds. Deep-fry a few at a time in hot oil for 2–3 minutes or bake for 10–12 minutes, until golden.

Oven preheated to 375°F/190°C

Preparation & cooking time 1–1¼ hours

Makes 20

Nutritional notes calories 128; protein 4g; carbohydrates 11g; total fat 8g, of which saturated fat 1g; fiber 0.1g; sodium 71mg

CHILI-MARINATED OLIVES

Marinating is an easy way of livening up plain olives. Try adding herbs or some finely grated lemon zest for interesting variations.

INGREDIENTS

1¼ cups (150g) pitted green olives
1 cup (100g) pitted black olives
4 tomatoes, peeled, seeded, and finely chopped (see page 39)
½ cup (120ml) vegetable oil
2 garlic cloves, crushed
1 tbsp tomato paste
1 tsp crushed red pepper flakes

1 In a small pan, cover the olives with cold water and bring to a boil. Drain the olives, rinse under cold water for a few seconds, then place back in the pan and cover with water again. Bring to a boil once more, then drain again and set aside.

2 Place all the remaining ingredients in a separate pan and simmer on low heat for 8–10 minutes. Add the olives, with ⅔ cup (150ml) water, and simmer over low heat until the water has been absorbed. Let cool, preferably overnight, but for at least a few hours.

3 To serve, spear the olives with toothpicks, which can be picked up by hand.

Preparation & cooking time 35 minutes, plus at least 4 hours cooling time

Serves 10

Nutritional notes calories 141; protein 0.6g; carbohydrates 1.3g; total fat 15g, of which saturated fat 2g; fiber 1g; sodium 573mg

GUACAMOLE & CHEESE CHALUPAS

In Mexico, fried tortillas form the basis of an endless variety of snacks. They are often served piled high with wonderful contrasting ingredients and called "chalupas" (which means little boats). This version is topped with tangy guacamole mixed with goat cheese.

INGREDIENTS

vegetable oil, for deep-frying

4 corn tortillas, 4½ inches (12cm) each, quartered

1 large avocado

¼ lb (125g) firm goat cheese, grated

½ red onion, diced

1 tsp cumin seeds

3 tsp lemon juice

Tabasco, to taste

salt and freshly ground pepper

6 tbsp plain yogurt, to serve

1 tbsp chopped fresh cilantro, to garnish

1 Heat the oil in a large skillet or deep-fat fryer. When hot, deep-fry the tortillas for 2 minutes until crisp and golden. Alternatively, you can bake the tortillas for 20 minutes.

2 Mash together the avocado and goat cheese. Add the onion, cumin seeds, lemon juice, Tabasco, and seasoning.

3 Top each tortilla with the guacamole, then a little yogurt. Sprinkle the cilantro on top, to garnish.

Oven preheated to 350°F/180°C

Preparation & cooking time 20–25 minutes

Makes 24

Nutritional notes calories 90; protein 3g; carbohydrates 7g; total fat 6g, of which saturated fat 2g; fiber 0.6g; sodium 91mg

EGG SALAD & WATERCRESS CROUTES

Egg salad and watercress is a great sandwich filling that we probably all take for granted, but serving it warm on toasted baguettes gives a new twist to this classic combination.

INGREDIENTS

5 hard-boiled eggs, finely chopped

1 bunch scallions, finely chopped

1 small bunch watercress, finely chopped

4 tbsp good-quality mayonnaise

2 tbsp freshly grated Parmesan

4 mini baguettes, sliced and toasted

salt and freshly ground pepper

1 Place the hard-boiled eggs in a medium bowl and mix in the remaining ingredients. Season to taste and chill until needed.

2 Spoon the egg mixture onto the bread. Broil until golden.

—VARIATION—

Brie & Mushroom Croûtes
Heat 1 tablespoon olive oil and sauté 2 crushed garlic cloves with ½ teaspoon fresh thyme leaves until soft. Add 1 cup (200g) chopped mushrooms and cook over high heat for 8–10 minutes. Stir in 1 tablespoon balsamic vinegar; simmer for 2 minutes. Top each toast piece with a slice of Brie and the mushrooms; broil as above.

Preparation & cooking time 15 minutes

Makes 24

Nutritional notes calories 119; protein 4g; carbohydrates 11g; total fat 7g, of which saturated fat 1g; fiber 0.4g; sodium 177mg

Asian Mushroom Sushi Purses

Chili-marinated Olives

Guacamole & Cheese Chalupas

Brie & Mushroom Croûtes

Egg Salad & Watercress Croûtes

SOUPS

SOUP HAS BEEN POPULAR throughout the ages. It can be made from any vegetable, enhanced with exotic spices and other flavorings, fresh herbs, grains, and beans. Soup is a comforting food in winter; a thick broth needs little more than some crusty bread to accompany it. For warmer days there are lighter and more delicate consommés: soups that can be served hot and some that can be served chilled. Here you will see how versatile soups can be, and how quick and easy they are to prepare.

LAZY CARIBBEAN SOUP

KEY INGREDIENTS

Passion fruit has an intense flavor and a lovely sweetness: the pulp and seeds are edible

Mango and galia melons are deliciously sweet, and ripe ones should be firm, but yielding

Red chilies bring a dash of color and spice to any dish

Lime accentuates flavors like lemon, but it is a little more sour

Fresh ginger adds a delicious pungency to dishes with its distinct spiciness

Maple syrup, made from the sap of the maple tree, is smooth and rich

Cilantro has a distinct aromatic quality and is excellent in salsas

What could be lazier – or more welcome – on a hot summer's day than a soup that does not require any cooking? All that is needed is a little chopping and blending, followed by an hour or so of chilling. Be sure to use well-ripened fruit for this recipe.

INGREDIENTS

4 passion fruit, halved
1 ripe mango, diced
1 inch (2.5cm) piece of fresh ginger, grated
2 tbsp maple syrup (or corn syrup)
1¼ cups (300ml) fresh orange juice
½ tsp cracked black pepper

FOR THE SALSA

½ mango, cut into ¼ inch (5mm) dice
1 small wedge of galia melon, cut into ¼ inch (5mm) dice
¼ avocado, cut into ¼ inch (5mm) dice
1 tomato, peeled, seeded, and chopped (see page 39)
1 small red onion, finely chopped
2 red chilies, seeded and thinly sliced
2 tbsp chopped fresh cilantro
pinch of cayenne
zest and juice of 2 limes

1 Scoop out the seeds from the passion fruit into a bowl. Add the mango and ginger, cover, and let marinate for 1 hour at room temperature.

2 Meanwhile, for the salsa, blend together all the ingredients in a bowl; set aside.

3 Place the passion fruit, mango, and ginger in a blender or food processor and add the maple syrup and orange juice. Blend to a fine puree, then strain through a fine strainer or sieve into a bowl. Cover and chill for 2 hours in the refrigerator.

4 To serve, add the salsa to the blended soup, sprinkle with a little cracked black pepper, and serve in individual, well-chilled bowls.

Preparation time
20 minutes, plus 1 hour marinating time, plus 2 hours chilling time

Serves 4

Nutritional notes
calories 144; protein 2g; carbohydrates 30g; total fat 2g, of which saturated fat 0.5g; fiber 3g; sodium 29mg

EARLY SUMMER BASIL SOUP

The better the quality of the basil, the better this simple, yet sophisticated, soup will be. Try to buy one of the large bunches of basil with a heady scent and pungent, peppery leaves that are sold loose in markets or Italian delicatessens.

INGREDIENTS

3 tbsp (50g) butter
1lb (400g) young leeks, roughly chopped
2 celery stalks, roughly chopped
5 cups (1.2 liters) Vegetable Stock (see page 44)
zest and juice of ½ lemon
leaves from 1 large bunch fresh basil, plus extra, to garnish
6 tbsp heavy cream, plus extra, to serve
salt and freshly ground pepper

1 Heat the butter in a large pan, add the leeks and celery, cover, and sweat for 5–10 minutes over medium heat. Remove the lid. Add the stock and lemon zest and juice. Bring to a boil, reduce the heat, and simmer for 15 minutes.

2 Remove from the heat, add the basil, and blend in a blender or food processor until smooth. Chill for 1 hour. Stir in the cream and adjust the seasoning. Serve chilled, with a generous swirl of cream, and garnish with basil leaves.

Preparation & cooking time
40 minutes, plus 1 hour for the stock, plus 1 hour chilling time

Serves 4

Nutritional notes
calories 354; protein 3g; carbohydrates 5g; total fat 36g, of which saturated fat 23g; fiber 2g; sodium 223mg

— CHICKPEA & SWISS CHARD MINESTRONE WITH PESTO —

Make this soup in the midst of summer, when basil is plentiful and well flavored.

INGREDIENTS

2 tbsp olive oil
1 onion, chopped
2 celery stalks, chopped
2 garlic cloves, crushed
½ tsp dried oregano
1 carrot, diced
½ cup (50g) Swiss chard, chopped
4½ cups (1 liter) Dark Vegetable Stock, (see page 44)
¾ cup (200g) canned crushed tomatoes
¼ tsp crushed red pepper flakes
2oz (50g) spaghetti
1 zucchini, diced
½ cup (50g) green beans, thinly sliced
1 potato, diced
½ cup (50g) frozen peas
1 cup (125g) canned chickpeas, drained

FOR THE PESTO

2 cups (75g) basil leaves
2 garlic cloves
1 tbsp pine nuts
2 tbsp freshly grated Parmesan
pinch of granulated sugar
⅓ cup (75ml) extra virgin olive oil
salt and freshly ground pepper

1 For the pesto, place all the ingredients except the olive oil in a blender or food processor and blend until smooth. With the motor still running, slowly add the oil until the pesto is smooth and has a grainy, slightly runny texture. Season to taste.

2 For the minestrone, heat the oil in a heavy-bottomed pan. Add the onion, celery, garlic, and oregano. Sauté over medium heat for 2–3 minutes, until soft. Add the carrot and chard and cook for 1 minute, until the chard has wilted.

3 Stir in the stock, tomatoes, and red pepper flakes, and bring to a boil. Reduce the heat and simmer for 50–60 minutes. Break the spaghetti into 1 inch (2.5cm) lengths and add to the soup with the zucchini, green beans, potato, peas, and chickpeas. Simmer over medium heat for 15 minutes, stirring occasionally, until the vegetables are tender.

4 Pour the soup into four individual serving bowls. Place a tablespoon of the pesto in each bowl and serve hot.

Preparation & cooking time
1¾ hours, plus 1 hour for the stock

Serves 4

Nutritional notes
calories 432; protein 11g; carbohydrates 31g; total fat 30g, of which saturated fat 5g; fiber 5g; sodium 285mg

PARSNIP & WILD RICE MULLIGATAWNY

Parsnips, curry spices, and apples are one of those unexpectedly delicious combinations that just work perfectly together. The wild rice gives a wonderful texture and body to this complex and sustaining soup.

INGREDIENTS

⅓ cup (50g) wild rice

3 tbsp (50g) butter

1 onion, chopped

1 garlic clove, crushed

1lb (450g) parsnips, diced

½ tsp turmeric

2 tbsp curry powder

5⅔ cups (1.5 liters) Vegetable Stock
(see page 44)

1 green apple, peeled and diced

½ cup (125ml) unsweetened
coconut milk

4 tbsp chopped fresh cilantro leaves

salt and freshly ground pepper

1 Place the wild rice in a large pan. Add 2 cups (450ml) of water, or enough to cover the rice, bring to a boil, reduce the heat, and simmer for 30–40 minutes, until the rice is tender. Drain.

2 Heat the butter in a separate pot. Add the onion and garlic and cook over low heat for 5 minutes, until soft. Add the parsnips, turmeric, and curry powder and cook for 2–3 minutes longer, to allow the spices to release their fragrances.

3 Pour in the stock and add the diced apple. Stir well, then simmer for 40 minutes, until the parsnips are tender.

4 Puree the ingredients until smooth in a blender or food processor. Strain through a coarse strainer or sieve, and season to taste. Return the soup to the pan and stir in the coconut milk, reserving 4 tablespoons. Bring almost to the boiling point, remove from the heat, and stir in the wild rice and cilantro. Serve with a swirl of reserved coconut milk.

🕐 **Preparation & cooking time**
1¾ hours, plus 1 hour for the stock

◎ **Serves 4**

♡ **Nutritional notes**
calories 251; protein 4g; carbohydrates 33g; total fat 12g, of which saturated fat 7g; fiber 7g; sodium 257mg

POTATO, SPINACH & SAFFRON SOUP

Here, fresh spinach and potatoes are cooked in a saffron-infused broth. Quail's eggs are then poached directly in the broth for an elegant presentation.

INGREDIENTS

7 cups (1.5 liters) Vegetable Stock
(see page 44) or water

2 pinches of saffron

¾ lb (250g) spinach leaves

2 tbsp olive oil

½ onion, chopped

1 garlic clove, crushed

3 small new potatoes,
peeled and sliced

salt and freshly cracked pepper

freshly grated nutmeg

4 quail's eggs

1 Pour the stock into a large pot, sprinkle in the saffron, and bring to a boil. Reduce the heat and simmer for 10 minutes to infuse the stock with the saffron. Remove from the heat.

2 Blanch the spinach leaves in a pot of boiling, salted water for 2 minutes, then immediately refresh in ice water. Drain and squeeze out any excess moisture.

3 Heat the oil in a pot, add the onion and garlic, and sweat over medium heat for 2–3 minutes, until soft. Stir in the spinach and cook for 2 minutes. Pour in the stock and bring to a boil. Add the potatoes, reduce the heat, and simmer for 15–20 minutes, until the potatoes are tender. Season with salt, pepper, and nutmeg.

4 Crack the eggs into the soup, making sure that there is room between each one. Poach the eggs for 1 minute until set. Ladle the soup into individual bowls, adding a poached egg to each bowl.

🕐 **Preparation & cooking time**
1 hour, plus 1 hour for the stock

◎ **Serves 4**

♡ **Nutritional notes**
calories 145; protein 6g; carbohydrates 13g; total fat 9g, of which saturated fat 2g; fiber 2g; sodium 222mg

Grilled Vegetable Gazpacho

GRILLED VEGETABLE GAZPACHO

Serve this soup as is for a rustic, smoky flavor, or stir in a spoonful of mayonnaise or heavy cream just before serving. Ketchup adds extra sweetness, but you can substitute a tablespoon of tomato paste if you prefer.

INGREDIENTS

1 lb (400g) ripe, but firm, plum tomatoes

1 red pepper, halved and seeded

1 green pepper, halved and seeded

1 red onion, cut into ¼ inch (5mm) rings

6 tbsp olive oil

2 slices white bread, soaked in water for 10 minutes, then squeezed out

½ cucumber, chopped

2 garlic cloves, sliced

2 tbsp red wine vinegar

1 tbsp fresh oregano leaves

4 fresh basil leaves, plus extra, to garnish

¼ tsp ground cumin

salt and freshly ground pepper

½ tsp granulated sugar

3 tbsp tomato ketchup

croutons, to serve

1 Brush the tomatoes, peppers, and onion with 2 tablespoons of the olive oil. Preheat the broiler to hot and broil the vegetables for 10 minutes, turning occasionally, until lightly charred all over; cool.

2 When cold, dice the vegetables. Place in a large bowl, reserving 2 tablespoons. Crumble the bread into the bowl, then add the cucumber, garlic, vinegar, 1¼ cups (300ml) water, herbs, cumin, and the remaining oil. Season, add the sugar and ketchup, and marinate for at least 6 hours in the refrigerator.

3 Blend to a fine puree in a blender or food processor. Strain through a coarse strainer. Serve well chilled, in individual bowls, with the reserved vegetables and a few croutons sprinkled on top. Garnish with basil leaves.

Preparation & cooking time
40 minutes, plus at least 6 hours marinating time (preferably overnight)

Serves 4

Nutritional notes
calories 127; protein 5g; carbohydrates 26g; total fat 1g, of which saturated fat 0.3g; fiber 4g; sodium 390mg

BUTTERNUT SOUP WITH CINNAMON CREAM

With its sweet, nutty flavor and smooth texture, butternut squash can be used to make one of the best winter soups. Serve the soup hot, and top each serving with a dollop of orange- and cinnamon-scented cream for a sophisticated finish.

INGREDIENTS

2 tbsp olive oil

1 onion, finely chopped

1½ lb (750g) butternut squash, peeled and chopped

1 carrot, chopped

1½ inch (4cm) piece of fresh ginger, grated

½ tsp ground cinnamon

1 tbsp ground coriander

3¼ cups (700ml) Vegetable Stock (see page 44)

1¼ cups (300ml) milk

2 tbsp semolina

salt and freshly ground pepper

FOR THE CINNAMON CREAM

½ cup (100ml) heavy cream

1 tsp grated orange zest

1 tsp ground cinnamon

1 In a heavy-bottomed pan, heat the olive oil and cook the onion over medium heat for 5 minutes, until golden. Add the squash, carrot, ginger, cinnamon, and coriander. Sauté over medium heat, stirring, for 5–8 minutes, until the vegetables are browned.

2 Add the stock and milk and bring to a boil. Reduce the heat to medium, stir in the semolina, and cook, stirring, for 30–35 minutes, until the vegetables are tender. Blend until smooth in a blender or food processor. Season.

3 For the cinnamon cream, lightly whisk together the cream, orange zest, and cinnamon until the mixture forms soft peaks. Serve the soup hot, topped with a spoonful of cinnamon cream.

Preparation & cooking time
1¼ hours, plus 1 hour for the stock

Serves 4

Nutritional notes
calories 327; protein 7g; carbohydrates 31g; total fat 21g, of which saturated fat 10g; fiber 4g; sodium 165mg

ROASTED CARROT SOUP WITH THAI FLAVORS

Thai flavorings, such as lemongrass, ginger, and cilantro, can transform the humble carrot into an exotic treat. Try this recipe using parsnips instead of carrots — it will work equally well.

INGREDIENTS

6 tbsp vegetable oil
1lb (450g) carrots, diced
2 tbsp (25g) butter
1 onion, chopped
2 garlic cloves, chopped
1 inch (2.5cm) piece of fresh ginger, chopped
1 stick lemongrass, finely chopped
1 red chili, finely sliced
1/2 tsp curry powder
1 tsp coriander seeds
1¾ cups (400ml) canned coconut milk
3¾ cups (700ml) Vegetable Stock (see page 44)
salt and freshly ground pepper
2 tbsp lime juice
2 tbsp chopped fresh cilantro

1 Heat the oil in an ovenproof dish and roast the carrots for 20–25 minutes, until lightly golden and tender. Set aside.

2 Melt the butter in a large pan, add the onion, garlic, ginger, lemongrass, chili, curry powder, and coriander, and cook over low heat for 5 minutes to allow the spices to release their fragrances.

3 Stir in the roasted carrots, coconut milk, and stock and bring to a boil. Reduce the heat to low and simmer gently for 8–10 minutes. Remove from the heat and season to taste. Add the lime juice and cilantro and stir well. Serve hot.

Oven preheated to 400°F/200°C

Preparation & cooking time 50 minutes, plus 1 hour for the stock

Serves 4

Nutritional notes calories 275; protein 2g; carbohydrates 18g; total fat 22g, of which saturated fat 5g; fiber 3g; sodium 287mg

BLACK BEAN SOUP WITH CHILI SOFRITO

This thick, inky soup is served with a vivid splash of chunky green relish. As well as being perfect for soups, black beans make delicious additions to salads. They also can be mashed and served in tortillas with a spicy salsa.

INGREDIENTS

3 tbsp (50g) butter
1 onion, chopped
2 celery stalks, chopped
1 small leek, chopped
2 garlic cloves, crushed
1 bay leaf
1/2 tsp ground cumin
1/4 tsp aniseed
1 tbsp chopped fresh oregano
1lb (375g) dried black beans, soaked overnight (see page 41)
salt and freshly ground pepper
juice of 1 lemon
4 tbsp crème fraîche, to serve

FOR THE SOFRITO

2 tbsp olive oil
2 scallions, chopped
1 garlic clove, crushed
1/2 green pepper, cored, seeded, and chopped
¾ cup (150g) fresh cilantro, chopped
1 small green chili, halved and seeded

1 Heat the butter in a medium pan. Add the onion, celery, leek, and garlic and cook over medium heat for 5 minutes. Add the bay leaf, cumin, aniseed, and oregano and reduce the heat to low. Cook the vegetables for 10–12 minutes, until tender.

2 Add the beans and 7 cups (1.5 liters) water and bring to a boil. Lower the heat, then simmer for 1¼–1½ hours, until the beans are tender.

3 Remove from the heat and puree in small batches in a blender or food processor until smooth. Add salt, pepper, and lemon juice to taste.

4 For the sofrito, blend all the ingredients to a coarse pulp in a blender or food processor. Season to taste. Serve the soup in hot bowls. Top each serving with a spoonful of crème fraîche and a generous spoonful of sofrito.

Preparation & cooking time 2¼ hours, plus overnight soaking time

Serves 4

Nutritional notes calories 474; protein 27g; carbohydrates 46g; total fat 20g, of which saturated fat 10g; fiber 2g; sodium 260mg

Chilled Cucumber & Bulgur Soup

The well-known Lebanese bulgur salad, tabbouleh, provided the inspiration for this refreshing chilled soup. Half the cucumber is lightly cooked to enhance its delicate flavor without destroying its freshness. The remaining cucumber is served raw in the tabbouleh topping.

INGREDIENTS

2 cucumbers, peeled, seeded, and chopped

2 tbsp (25g) butter

1 medium leek, sliced

1 garlic clove, crushed

1 tsp chopped fresh oregano, or ½ tsp dried

2 cups (450ml) Vegetable Stock (see page 44)

⅔ cup (150ml) heavy cream

⅔ cup (150ml) plain yogurt

1 tsp Dijon mustard

juice of ½ lemon

salt and freshly ground pepper

FOR THE TABBOULEH

½ cup (100g) bulgur

1 onion, chopped

2 tbsp chopped fresh flat-leaf parsley

2 tbsp chopped fresh mint

8 pitted black olives, finely chopped

4 tbsp lemon juice

4 tbsp olive oil

1 tomato, peeled, seeded (see page 39), and diced

1 For the tabbouleh, soak the bulgur in a bowl of cold water for 1 hour. Drain, then squeeze out any excess water. Spread out on a clean cloth to dry.

2 Put the cucumber in a bowl and sprinkle with salt. After 30 minutes, rinse and pat dry.

3 Heat the butter in a pan. Add the leek, half the cucumber, and the garlic. Sweat over medium heat for about 5 minutes. Add the oregano, stock, cream, and yogurt and blend in a blender or food processor. Add the remaining soup ingredients and blend until smooth. Strain and chill.

4 For the tabbouleh, mix the onion, parsley, mint, olives, and remaining cucumber in a bowl with the bulgur. Mix in the remaining ingredients, then season. Pile a tablespoon of tabbouleh in each bowl and ladle in the soup.

Preparation & cooking time
1 hour 40 minutes, plus 1 hour for the stock

Serves 4

Nutritional notes
calories 469; protein 7g; carbohydrates 28g; total fat 37g, of which saturated fat 17g; fiber 2g; sodium 393mg

Lebanese Green Lentil Soup with Mint Oil

This soup is a godsend to those who find that their homegrown mint annually runs riot and threatens to take over their whole garden. The mint oil is not only a nice addition to this soup but it also makes a good dressing for pasta or salad.

INGREDIENTS

2 tbsp olive oil

1 onion, chopped

2 garlic cloves, crushed

1 cup (250g) baby lentils, soaked for 3 hours

2 tbsp cumin seeds

½ tsp coriander seeds

¾ cup (200g) canned crushed tomatoes

½ tbsp tomato paste

5⅔ cups (1.5 liters) Vegetable Stock (see page 44)

juice of ½ lemon

salt and freshly ground pepper

pinch of cayenne

FOR THE MINT OIL

handful of fresh mint leaves

4 tbsp olive oil

1 Heat the oil in a pan, add the onion and garlic, and sweat over medium heat for 10 minutes, until soft. Add the lentils, cumin, and coriander seeds, and cook over medium heat for 5–10 minutes. Add the tomatoes, tomato paste, and stock. Bring to a boil, then reduce the heat and simmer for 40 minutes, until the lentils are soft.

2 Blend to a smooth puree in a blender or food processor. Stir in the lemon juice and season with salt, pepper, and cayenne.

3 For the mint oil, place the mint and olive oil in a blender or food processor and blend to a coarse puree. Serve the soup hot with a swirl of the mint oil on top.

Preparation & cooking time
1 hour 10 minutes, plus 3 hours soaking time, plus 1 hour for the stock

Serves 4

Nutritional notes
calories 361; protein 17g; carbohydrates 36g; total fat 19g, of which saturated fat 3g; fiber 7g; sodium 138mg

SMOKY CORN VELOUTE

You will need fresh corn on the cob for this recipe. You can broil it under the broiler or grill it on a barbecue for that uniquely smoky taste. To enhance the flavor of the stock, even the cobs are used in this recipe.

INGREDIENTS

4 ears corn on the cob

7 cups (1.5 liters) Vegetable Stock (see page 44)

2 tbsp olive oil

3 tbsp (40g) butter

1 onion, chopped

1 garlic clove, crushed

1 leek, chopped

4 corn tortillas, chopped

salt and freshly ground pepper

TO FINISH THE SOUP

½ cup (100ml) heavy cream, plus extra, to serve

1 egg yolk

¾ cup (75g) coarsely grated Cheddar

2 corn tortillas, cut into strips and deep-fried

1 Broil the corn under a hot broiler for 10 minutes, turning them until charred, but not burned.

2 Scrape off the kernels with a knife and reserve. Chop the cobs and place in a pot. Cover with the stock, bring to a boil, reduce the heat, and simmer for 45 minutes. Strain the stock and set aside; discard the cobs.

3 Heat the oil and butter in a pan. Add the onion, garlic, leek, and tortillas and cook over medium heat for 3–4 minutes. Reduce the heat and add the corn kernels. Pour in the stock and simmer for 45 minutes, stirring often. Blend until smooth in a blender or food processor. Season.

4 To finish the soup, gently whisk together the cream and egg yolk. Add one ladleful of soup, whisk, then return to the pan. Heat through, then transfer to four bowls. Top each bowl with Cheddar, fried tortilla strips, and a swirl of cream.

Preparation & cooking time
2¼ hours, plus 1 hour for the stock

Serves 4

Nutritional notes
calories 694; protein 18g; carbohydrates 77g; total fat 37g, of which saturated fat 19g; fiber 6g; sodium 545mg

Note: this recipe contains lightly cooked egg.

Hot & Sour Vegetable Soup

In China, soup is a very important part of any meal, and this particular soup is one of the most popular. You may need to go to an Asian food store to buy the dried Chinese mushrooms, but all the other ingredients are available in supermarkets. The white wine vinegar adds the sour note to the soup.

INGREDIENTS

2 tbsp sesame oil

8 scallions, sliced

1 cup (150g) carrots, finely shredded

1 inch (2.5cm) piece of fresh ginger, finely shredded

1 garlic clove, crushed

3¼ cups (700ml) Dark Vegetable Stock (see page 44)

4 dried Chinese black mushrooms

1 bok choy, shredded

4 tbsp ketjap manis (Indonesian soy sauce)

2 tbsp white wine vinegar

1 tsp superfine sugar

1 tsp chili oil

1 tbsp cornstarch, mixed to a paste with 2 tbsp cold water

1 egg, lightly beaten

2oz (50g) firm tofu, cut into ¼ inch (5mm) cubes

1 Heat the sesame oil in a large pan over high heat until hot, then add half the scallions, the carrots, ginger, and garlic. Reduce the heat to medium and cook, stirring, for 5 minutes. Add the stock and bring to a boil. Add the dried Chinese black mushrooms and simmer for 10 minutes, then add the bok choy.

2 In a bowl, combine the ketjap manis with the vinegar, sugar, chili oil, and cornstarch paste. Mix together to form a paste.

3 Add the mixture to the soup, stir it, and bring to a boil. Boil for 1 minute. Gradually add the beaten egg to the soup, stirring gently so that it forms thin strands. Add the tofu, scatter the remaining scallions on top, and serve hot.

Preparation & cooking time
40 minutes, plus 1 hour for the stock

Serves 4

Nutritional notes
calories 178; protein 6g; carbohydrates 19g; total fat 9g, of which saturated fat 1g; fiber 2g; sodium 901mg

Roasted Red Pepper & Zhug Soup

Zhug is a fiery hot relish from Yemen, made with cilantro, garlic, and masses of chili. It is usually served as an accompaniment to grilled food, but here it forms the base of this vivid soup.

INGREDIENTS

4 red peppers, roasted, peeled, and seeded (see page 39)

2½ cups (600ml) Vegetable Stock (see page 44)

⅔ cup (150ml) tomato passata

4 tbsp fresh cilantro leaves

salt and freshly ground pepper

1 tbsp balsamic vinegar

1 tbsp honey

FOR THE ZHUG

3 garlic cloves, roughly chopped

½ tsp coriander seeds

½ tsp cumin seeds

2 red chilies, halved and seeded

4 tbsp olive oil

1 large onion, grated

1 For the zhug, dry roast the garlic, coriander, cumin, and chilies in a dry skillet over low heat, for 5 minutes. Add the oil, stir in the onion, and continue to cook for 10 minutes longer. Set aside to cool.

2 Place the zhug in a blender or food processor. Add the roasted peppers, 6 tablespoons of the vegetable stock, the passata, and the fresh cilantro, and blend to a puree.

3 Place the puree in a large pot and heat through over medium heat, stirring occasionally. Stir in the remaining vegetable stock and season to taste with salt and pepper. Finally, add the vinegar and honey. Stir the soup well and serve hot.

Preparation & cooking time
1 hour, plus 1 hour for the stock

Serves 4

Nutritional notes
calories 200; protein 3g; carbohydrates 21g; total fat 12g, of which saturated fat 2g; fiber 4g; sodium 109mg

TARTS & PIES

ORIGINALLY CONCEIVED for convenience, the wrapping of food in pastry or dough has been elevated to an art form. These recipes demonstrate the versatility of pastry, from crispy phyllo to delicate brioche dough and buttery short crust.

They show how pastry can be combined with the exciting flavors and textures of fresh green leaves, succulent roasted vegetables, herbs, cheeses, and spices. Any of these dishes will make a centerpiece for a special meal or for an informal family dinner.

SPINACH, BASIL & PUMPKIN RICE TORTE

KEY INGREDIENTS

Phyllo pastry is available in thin sheets and has a light, delicate texture

Spinach is flavorful and colorful; it is ideal with cream or cheese

Parmesan with risotto is a classic combination

Arborio, the risotto rice, comes from Piedmont, northern Italy

Pumpkin lends sweetness and color to many dishes

Fresh basil gives the true taste of Italian cuisine

This recipe is a variation on a classic Italian staple, Torta de Riso, or Rice Tart, which originated in Piedmont. I truly love the simplicity and rustic character of this dish. There are many variations throughout Italy. My favorite includes layers of sliced, hard-boiled eggs and slices of mozzarella between the layers of rice. Serve warm with Roasted Cherry Tomato Salsa (see page 45).

INGREDIENTS

2 tbsp olive oil
1 onion, thinly sliced
1lb (400g) fresh spinach
handful of fresh basil leaves, chopped
1 cup (200g) arborio rice, cooked
1 cup (100g) grated Parmesan
2 eggs, lightly beaten
3 tbsp (50g) butter, melted
9 sheets phyllo pastry, halved
1½lb (625g) pumpkin, peeled, cut into ½ inch (1cm) slices, and boiled
salt and freshly ground pepper

1 Heat the oil in a pan and cook the onion over medium to low heat for 5 minutes, until golden. Add the spinach and basil and cook for 2 minutes, until wilted. Finely chop, then place in a dish towel and squeeze out the excess moisture. Divide the rice equally between two bowls, add the

spinach to one, and divide the Parmesan and eggs between the two bowls. Mix well.

2 Grease an 8 inch (20cm) springform cake pan with butter. Brush the sheets of phyllo pastry with butter and use to line the bottom and sides of the cake pan, leaving a small overhang of phyllo. Reserve six half-sheets of phyllo for the top (keep under a damp cloth until ready to use).

3 Layer the torte: place the spinach rice in the bottom, followed by the pumpkin, with the remaining rice on top; season each layer. Cut the reserved pastry into strips, brush with butter, and use to decorate the torte. Bake for 50 minutes, until golden. Turn out of the pan onto a baking sheet and bake for a few minutes longer to crisp the sides. Cool a little before serving.

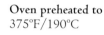

Oven preheated to 375°F/190°C

Preparation & cooking time 1½–1¾ hours

Serves 8

Nutritional notes calories 210; protein 10g; carbohydrates 11g; total fat 14g, of which saturated fat 7g; fiber 2g; sodium 384mg

SALSIFY & WILD MUSHROOM TART

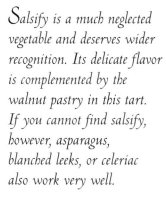

Salsify is a much neglected vegetable and deserves wider recognition. Its delicate flavor is complemented by the walnut pastry in this tart. If you cannot find salsify, however, asparagus, blanched leeks, or celeriac also work very well.

INGREDIENTS

FOR THE WALNUT PASTRY

2¼ cups (250g) all-purpose flour

pinch of salt

½ cup (60g) ground walnuts

9 tbsp (135g) unsalted butter, chilled and cut into cubes, plus extra, to grease

1 egg, beaten

FOR THE FILLING

juice of ½ lemon

1½ cups (150g) salsify, peeled and cut diagonally into ¾ inch (2cm) lengths

2 tbsp (25g) butter

¼ lb (100g) oyster mushrooms, chopped

1 cup (50g) sliced porcini mushrooms, soaked overnight in ½ cup (125ml) water

½ cup (120ml) heavy cream

1 egg, beaten

1 tbsp chopped fresh flat leaf parsley

salt and freshly ground pepper

selection of mâche and curly endive, to serve

FOR THE MUSTARD VINAIGRETTE

3 tbsp olive oil

1 tbsp walnut oil

1 tbsp champagne or white wine vinegar

1 tsp whole grain mustard

1 tbsp red currant jelly

1 For the pastry, sift the flour and salt into a bowl and mix in the walnuts. Rub in the butter until the mixture resembles fine bread crumbs. Stir in the egg to bind. Gather the pastry together and roll into a ball, cover, and let chill for 1 hour.

2 For the filling, bring a large pot of water to a boil, add the lemon juice, and poach the salsify for 4–5 minutes. Drain.

3 Heat the butter in a skillet and fry the oyster mushrooms over medium heat for 2–3 minutes until tender. Drain the porcini, reserving the soaking liquid, and add the porcini to the pan. Season lightly and set aside. Mix together the cream, egg, parsley, and reserved porcini soaking liquid. Season to taste and set aside.

4 Roll out the pastry on a lightly floured work surface and use to line four lightly greased, individual 3 inch (7cm) tart pans. Prick the bottoms with a fork, cover with waxed paper, and fill with baking beans. Bake blind for 5–6 minutes. Remove the beans and paper, and let cool.

5 Arrange the salsify and mushrooms in the bottoms of the tart shells, then pour in the cream mixture to fill each shell. Bake for 12–15 minutes, until the pastry is golden and the filling has just set.

6 For the vinaigrette, blend all the ingredients together well. Arrange a bed of mâche and curly endive on each of four serving plates and drizzle with the vinaigrette. Place one tart on top of each bed of greens and serve while still warm.

Oven preheated to 400°F/200°C

Preparation & cooking time 2 hours, plus overnight soaking time

Serves 4

Nutritional notes calories 953; protein 15g; carbohydrates 63g; total fat 73g, of which saturated fat 34g; fiber 4g; sodium 597mg

HIGH-RISE PASTA PIE

This impressive pasta pie first caught my eye in Italy, where it was filled with pasta bound in a thick ragu sauce (tomato and meat-based sauce). I experimented with the recipe and have come up with my own vegetarian version. It is great for an informal buffet-style lunch or a dinner party and tastes equally good served hot or cold.

INGREDIENTS

1 batch Short Crust Pastry (see page 42)

½lb (225g) macaroni or penne pasta

3 tbsp (50g) butter, plus extra, to grease

¾lb (350g) Swiss chard leaves, roughly shredded

¼lb (125g) chestnut mushrooms, quartered

¾ cup (50g) sun-dried tomatoes, roughly chopped

2 tbsp (25g) pine nuts, toasted

½ cup (50g) frozen peas, defrosted

1 tbsp cornstarch or arrowroot, mixed to a paste with 2 tbsp cold water

1¼ cups (300ml) heavy cream

3 eggs, beaten

salt and freshly ground pepper

freshly grated nutmeg

1 Lightly grease an 8 inch (22cm) springform cake pan. On a lightly floured work surface, roll out two thirds of the pastry and use to line the cake pan.

2 Cook the pasta in plenty of boiling, salted water according to package instructions, until al dente. Drain and season with salt, pepper, and nutmeg.

3 Melt the butter in a large pan, add the chard, and sweat over medium heat for 4–5 minutes until tender. Add the mushrooms and tomatoes, and cook for 1 minute. Remove from the heat and toss together with the pasta. Add the pine nuts and peas, mix well, and adjust the seasoning.

4 Place the pasta in the pastry shell and press down lightly. Combine the cornstarch paste with the cream and eggs in a bowl, then pour the cream mixture over the pasta in the pan.

5 Roll out the remaining pastry into a circle large enough to cover the pie. Dampen the edges of the pastry with water, then top the pie with the pastry circle. Crimp and seal the edges by pressing with your thumb and forefinger all the way around. Score a criss-cross pattern on the top.

6 Make a small hole in the top for steam to escape. Bake for 1¼–1½ hours, until the pastry is golden and the middle is set. Let rest for 10–15 minutes before serving. Serve hot or cold.

Oven preheated to 375°F/190°C

Preparation & cooking time 2¼–2½ hours, plus 40 minutes for the pastry

Serves 8

Nutritional notes calories 836; protein 14g; carbohydrates 59g; total fat 62g, of which saturated fat 35g; fiber 3g; sodium 321mg

TUSCAN ROLL

Filled with roasted vegetables, mozzarella, sun-dried tomatoes, and olive paste, this colorful loaf is imbued with the irresistible flavors and aromas of Italy. Use a good olive oil for roasting the vegetables to give them a superb taste. You can make the Tuscan Roll ahead and freeze it, uncooked, for up to three months. Olivada is an olive spread, great for adding extra flavor to dishes.

Oven preheated to
400°F/200°C

Preparation &
cooking time
2 hours

Serves 8

Nutritional notes
calories 384; protein 11g;
carbohydrates 30g;
total fat 25g, of which
saturated fat 5g;
fiber 4g; sodium 629mg

INGREDIENTS

FOR THE DOUGH

2¼ cups (250g) unbleached white flour,
plus extra, to dust

¼oz (10g) sachet easy-blend yeast

½ tsp salt

⅔ cup (150ml) lukewarm water

1 tbsp olive oil, plus extra, to grease

FOR THE FILLING

1 eggplant, cut into ½ inch (1cm) slices

1 onion, sliced

4 zucchini (2 yellow, 2 green) cut
into ½ inch (1cm) slices

2 medium fennel, cut into wedges

6 tbsp olive oil

1½ cups (150g) sun-dried tomatoes

4 tbsp olivada (see page 45)

2 garlic cloves, crushed

¾ lb (300g) Swiss chard or spinach

¼ lb (125g) mozzarella,
thinly sliced

salt and freshly ground pepper

1 For the dough, stir together the flour, yeast, and salt in a large mixing bowl. Make a well in the center and pour in the water and oil. Mix until all the liquid has been absorbed. Knead the dough on a lightly floured work surface for 2–3 minutes until smooth and elastic.

2 Place the dough in an oiled bowl, cover with a cloth, and leave in a warm place until doubled in size, about 20–25 minutes.

3 For the filling, place the eggplant, onion, zucchini, and fennel in a roasting pan, in separate rows. Drizzle with 4 tablespoons of oil, season with salt and pepper, and bake for 25–30 minutes, until tender. Place half the sun-dried tomatoes in a blender or food processor and blend to a coarse puree. Mix with the olivada.

4 Heat the remaining oil in a pan and cook the garlic and Swiss chard for 3–4 minutes, until wilted. Let cool. Place in a clean dish towel and squeeze out any excess moisture.

5 On a lightly floured work surface, roll out the dough into a rectangle measuring 10 inches x 8 inches (25cm x 20cm). Spread the olivada mixture over the dough, leaving a 1 inch (2.5cm) border all around. Lay half the eggplant on top, followed by the chard, then the fennel, the remaining sun-dried tomatoes, mozzarella, zucchini, and finally, the remaining eggplant. Season each layer.

6 Fold the two short edges of the dough over the filling. With the long edge toward you, roll the dough up to enclose the filling. Place seam side down on a greased baking sheet. Bake for 30–35 minutes, until golden. Let cool completely before cutting into thick slices and serving.

CEPE, WALNUT & JERUSALEM ARTICHOKE PACKAGES

This is an elegant and tasty dish that can provide a solution to the annual challenge of what to serve for a vegetarian Christmas meal. You could try combinations of different vegetables, and perhaps replace the Cheddar with Gruyère or Parmesan, and the walnuts with hazelnuts or cashews. The variations on fillings are endless, so experiment.

INGREDIENTS

¾ cup (150g) long-grain brown rice

2 tbsp (25g) butter

2 shallots, finely chopped

1 garlic clove, crushed

1 large leek, shredded

½lb (175g) cepes or large mushrooms, sliced

¼lb (150g) Jerusalem artichokes, peeled and grated

1 tbsp chopped fresh thyme

4 fresh basil leaves, shredded

2½ cups (150g) fresh white bread crumbs

½ cup (50g) walnuts, chopped

¼lb (100g) Cheddar, grated

2 eggs, plus 1 to seal and glaze, beaten

salt and freshly ground pepper

pinch of nutmeg

1lb (450g) store-bought puff pastry, defrosted if frozen

flour, to dust

sprigs of fresh basil, to garnish

Madeira Sauce (see page 44), to serve

1 Boil the rice for 30–35 minutes, or according to package instructions, until tender. Drain, place in a bowl, and let cool.

2 In a separate pan, heat the butter, add the shallots and garlic, and sauté for 5 minutes over low heat until softened. Add the leek and, over high heat, stir in the cepes, artichokes, and herbs. Sauté for about 5 minutes, until golden. Let cool.

3 In a clean bowl, combine the rice, sautéed vegetables, bread crumbs, walnuts, Cheddar, and 2 eggs. Season to taste with salt, pepper, and nutmeg.

4 On a lightly floured work surface, roll out the pastry to a rectangle about ⅛ inch (3mm) thick. Trim to 12 inches x 8 inches (30cm x 20cm), then cut into six 4 inch (10cm) squares.

5 Form the rice mixture into balls, each about the size of a golf ball. Place one in the center of each pastry square, and form the packages (see steps 1–3 below).

6 Brush the outside of each package with beaten egg and leave in the refrigerator until ready to bake. Bake for 15–20 minutes, until golden. Garnish with basil and serve with Madeira sauce.

Oven preheated to 400°F/200°C

Preparation & cooking time 1½ hours, plus 1 hour for the Madeira sauce

Serves 6

Nutritional notes calories 705; protein 18g; carbohydrates 54g; total fat 48g, of which saturated fat 11g; fiber 3g; sodium 528mg

MAKING THE PACKAGES

1 Place a rice ball, about the size of a golf ball, in the center of each pastry square. Brush the edges of the square with beaten egg.

2 Bring the four corners up to the center, then press the edges together with your index fingers and thumbs to seal in the filling.

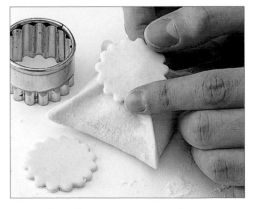

3 Roll out the pastry trimmings and cut out six circles, each about 1½ inches (4cm) in diameter. Place on the packages and press down lightly to seal.

PEPPER & DOLCELATTE TARTS

Dolcelatte and sage is an excellent combination, very popular in Italian cookery. With their multicolored topping of roasted pepper strips, these little tarts make an eye-catching appetizer or delicious light lunch.

INGREDIENTS

½ batch Short Crust Pastry
(see page 42)

5 tbsp olive oil, plus extra, to grease

2 red onions, thinly sliced

1 large garlic clove, crushed

1 tbsp chopped fresh sage

3 tbsp milk

3½oz (100g) dolcelatte or blue cheese

3 peppers (1 red, 1 green, 1 yellow)
roasted, peeled, seeded (see page 39),
and cut in julienne strips

¼ cup (25g) pitted black olives, sliced

salt and freshly cracked black pepper

1 Lightly grease four individual 3 inch (7cm) tart pans. Roll out the pastry on a lightly floured work surface and use to line the tart pans. Prick the bases, line with waxed paper, and fill with baking beans. Let the pastry rest in a cool place for 15 minutes before baking.

2 Bake the pastry shells blind for 5–6 minutes, remove the baking beans and paper, and return the shells to the oven for 3–4 minutes, until crisp. Let cool, then remove from the pans.

3 Heat 3 tablespoons of olive oil in a skillet and cook the onions, garlic, and sage over low heat for about 15 minutes until softened. Remove from the heat. Cream together the milk and the dolcelatte to make a thick sauce. Beat the cheese mixture into the onions until the cheese melts.

4 Season the mixture and divide it between the pastry shells, then arrange the roasted pepper strips on top, following the curve of the tarts. Dot with the olives, drizzle with the remaining oil, and sprinkle with pepper. Place on a baking sheet and return to the oven to heat through for 5 minutes, then serve warm.

Oven preheated to
375°F/190°C

Preparation & cooking time
1½ hours,
plus 40 minutes
for the pastry

Serves 4

Nutritional notes
calories 559; protein 10g;
carbohydrates 41g;
total fat 40g, of which
saturated fat 21g;
fiber 3g; sodium 402mg

POTATO, PEA & MINT TURNOVERS

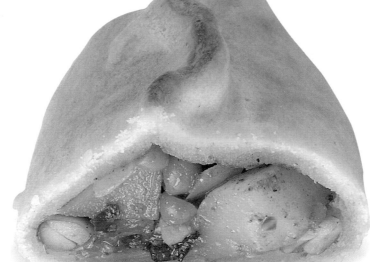

Chopped mint adds a refreshing note to the spicy filling in these little turnovers. They are perfect for parties and can be prepared well ahead of time. You can freeze them uncooked for up to three months, then bake or fry them frozen; just allow a few minutes longer for them to cook.

Oven preheated to
400°F/200°C

Preparation & cooking time
1½–2 hours

Serves 8

Nutritional notes
calories 280; protein 8g; carbohydrates 37g; total fat 12g, of which saturated fat 5g; fiber 3g; sodium 145mg

INGREDIENTS

FOR THE PASTRY DOUGH

2¼ cups (250g) all-purpose flour

3 tbsp (50g) chilled butter, cubed

⅓ cup (75ml) milk

1 egg, beaten, to glaze

FOR THE FILLING

3 tbsp vegetable oil, plus extra for deep-frying, plus extra, to grease

1 onion, chopped

1 garlic clove, crushed

½ tsp turmeric

1 tsp ground cumin

1 tsp garam masala

good pinch of ground ginger

½ tsp crushed red pepper flakes

2 medium potatoes, diced

1½ cups (150g) frozen peas

2 tbsp chopped fresh mint

salt and freshly ground pepper

fruit chutney or Tomato Raita (see page 147), to serve

1 For the pastry, sift the flour into a bowl, add the butter, and rub in until the mixture resembles fine bread crumbs. Mix in the milk to form a soft dough. Turn onto a lightly floured surface and knead. Wrap in oiled plastic wrap, and let chill in the refrigerator for 45 minutes.

2 For the filling, heat the oil in a skillet, add the onion, garlic, and spices, and cook gently for 3–4 minutes. In a separate pan, deep-fry the potatoes for about 5 minutes, until golden. Add the potatoes to the spices, and stir until well coated with the mixture.

3 Add boiling water to cover the mixture, reduce the heat, and simmer for 3–5 minutes. Add the peas and cook for 2–3 minutes longer. Remove from the heat, add the mint, season, and let cool.

4 Take the pastry out of the refrigerator and let it stand for 5 minutes before dividing it into eight pieces. On a lightly floured surface, roll each piece into a 5 inch (13cm) circle. Place a mound of filling in the center of each circle, brush the border with beaten egg, then bring the pastry up over the filling. Press the edges together to seal.

5 Brush the turnovers with the beaten egg, lay on a lightly greased baking sheet, and bake for 12–15 minutes. Alternatively, deep-fry them in hot oil for 5 minutes. Serve with a fruit chutney or tomato raita.

PASTA & GNOCCHI

THE ACT OF TRANSFORMING just a few simple ingredients into golden sheets of pasta can be immensely satisfying. However, some recipes call for dried, commercial pasta, such as penne. Always cook pasta and gnocchi in plenty of boiling, salted water, to which a little oil has been added to keep them from sticking. Gnocchi are little dumplings. They are usually made with potatoes, but here I have included some variations: gnocchi made with orange sweet potatoes, ricotta, and even olive bread.

—— LAYERED STRACCHI WITH ROASTED VEGETABLES ——

KEY INGREDIENTS

Red peppers are widely used for their color and sweet taste

Zucchini need hardly any cooking; the smaller they are the more flavor they have

Fresh pasta has a different texture than dried pasta — you can buy it, but it is worth making your own

Eggplants are popular in Mediterranean countries and combine well with acidic foods

Garlic, plum tomatoes, basil, and pine nuts are delicious in pesto and other Mediterranean sauces

Stracchi, which means "rags" in Italian, describes perfectly these sheets of pasta, layered loosely with vegetables. The pasta is served with a pesto made with roasted tomatoes, which provide a mellow flavor.

INGREDIENTS

1 batch basic pasta dough (see page 43)
1 onion, cut into ½ inch (1cm) rings
1 large eggplant, sliced
4 small tomatoes, halved
2 zucchini, sliced
4 tbsp olive oil
3 peppers (1 red, 1 yellow, 1 green), roasted, peeled, and seeded (see page 39)
fresh chives, to garnish

FOR THE ROASTED TOMATO PESTO

4 garlic cloves, peeled
⅔ cup (150ml) extra virgin olive oil
6 plum tomatoes, peeled (see page 39)
1 cup (25g) fresh basil leaves
2 tbsp (25g) pine nuts
2 tbsp freshly grated Parmesan
salt and freshly ground pepper

1 Roll out the dough into thin sheets (see page 43), and cut into 12 rectangles, each 4 inches x 3 inches (10cm x 7.5cm).

2 Set the pasta sheets aside and preheat the broiler. Brush all the vegetables except the peppers with some of the oil. Broil the oiled vegetables for 5 minutes on each side, until charred and tender.

3 For the pesto, drizzle the garlic with 1 tablespoon of olive oil and roast for 15 minutes. Roughly chop the tomatoes and add to the garlic. Roast for 15 minutes more.

4 Transfer the tomatoes and garlic to a blender or food processor. Puree with the remaining pesto ingredients. Season to taste and set aside.

5 Cook the pasta in boiling, salted water for 5 minutes, until al dente; drain. Layer all the vegetables and the pesto between three sheets of pasta per person. Drizzle with oil and a little more pesto, then garnish with chives.

Oven preheated to
400°F/200°C

Preparation & cooking time
1 hour, plus
30 minutes for
the pasta dough

Serves 4

Nutritional notes
calories 904; protein 20g;
carbohydrates 65g;
total fat 65g, of which
saturated fat 11g;
fiber 8g; sodium 230mg

BUCKWHEAT LASAGNETTE WITH CABBAGE & CEPES

This is quite a complex dish, which involves making your own buckwheat pasta. However, I think you will find that the taste repays the effort. The lasagnette has a nutty, autumnal flavor, which complements the cabbage, mushrooms, and sage in the filling perfectly.

INGREDIENTS

FOR THE LASAGNETTE

1½ cups (200g) buckwheat flour

1 cup (120g) unbleached flour, plus extra, to dust

2 eggs, plus 2 egg yolks, beaten together

2 tbsp olive oil

FOR THE FILLING

1 small Savoy cabbage, shredded

3 tbsp (50g) butter, plus extra, to grease

1 garlic clove, crushed

4 large fresh sage leaves

½lb (250g) cepes, sliced

salt and freshly ground pepper

freshly grated nutmeg

FOR THE SAUCE

1¾ cups (200g) grated Pecorino cheese

3 tbsp (50g) butter

⅔ cup (150ml) whipping cream

1 egg yolk

1 For the lasagnette, blend together the two flours on a clean surface. Make a well in the center, pour in the eggs and oil, and gradually incorporate the flour to form a dough.

2 Work the dough until it feels moist but not sticky. Place in a bowl, cover with plastic wrap, and let rest for 1 hour.

3 Roll out the pasta into thin sheets (see page 43). Cut into eight 8 inch (20cm) squares, then set aside on a floured baking sheet to dry for about 10 minutes.

4 For the filling, blanch the cabbage for 3 minutes in boiling water; drain well. Heat the butter in a skillet, then add the garlic and sage leaves. Add the cepes and the blanched cabbage and cook over medium heat for 4–5 minutes. Season with salt, pepper, and nutmeg.

5 Cook the pasta in boiling, salted water until al dente; drain. Season with salt, pepper, and nutmeg. Lay out the pasta on a flat work surface, spread with the cabbage and mushroom mixture, and roll each sheet up tightly. Cut each roll into small, equal-size slices, and lay these flat in a lightly buttered, ovenproof dish. Set aside.

6 For the sauce, place the Pecorino, butter, and cream in a large, heatproof bowl over a pan of boiling water. Melt the Pecorino slowly, whisking occasionally. Season, add the egg yolk, and whisk until the sauce is smooth. Pour the sauce over the lasagnette. Bake for 15 minutes, until golden.

Oven preheated to 400°F/200°C

Preparation & cooking time 1¼ hours, plus 1 hour resting time

Serves 4

Nutritional notes calories 1000; protein 37g; carbohydrates 70g; total fat 66g, of which saturated fat 36g; fiber 5g; sodium 904mg

OLIVADA & MOZZARELLA STUFFED EGGPLANT

Stuffing eggplant slices with tagliatelle is easier than might be expected, as long as you use a two-pronged fork, such as a carving fork. Take a few pasta strands, roll them around the fork into a neat shape, then ease this off onto a slice of eggplant.
If the pasta starts to stick before it is rolled, toss it in a little olive oil.

INGREDIENTS

6oz (175g) fresh tagliatelle (see page 43)

salt and freshly ground pepper

freshly grated nutmeg

6 tbsp olive oil

1 garlic clove, crushed

2 eggplants, thinly sliced lengthwise

4 tbsp Olivada (see page 45)

1½ cups (150g) grated mozzarella

handful of fresh basil leaves, shredded, plus extra, to garnish

⅔ cup (150ml) Fresh Tomato Sauce (see page 45), optional

1 Bring a large pot of salted water to a boil and cook the tagliatelle for 3 minutes, until al dente. Drain well and return to the pot. Season with salt, pepper, and nutmeg, then let cool.

2 Heat the oil in a skillet, then add the garlic and eggplant slices. Cook the eggplant over medium heat for 5 minutes on each side, until golden and tender. Drain any excess oil from the eggplant on paper towels.

3 Lay the eggplant slices on a chopping board, spread each one with olivada, and top with grated mozzarella.

4 Roll a forkful of the cooked tagliatelle into a ball and place on top of the mozzarella. Sprinkle with the shredded basil leaves. Roll up each eggplant slice and secure with a toothpick.

5 Arrange the eggplant rolls in a single layer in a baking dish, and bake for 10–12 minutes. Transfer to a serving dish and add the tomato sauce, if using. Garnish with fresh basil.

Oven preheated to 350°F/180°C

Preparation & cooking time
1 hour, plus 40 minutes to make the tagliatelle

Serves 4

Nutritional notes
calories 562; protein 18g; carbohydrates 32g; total fat 41g, of which saturated fat 10g; fiber 5g; sodium 638mg

PASTA WITH TOMATO, OLIVE & MELON SALSA

This is a wonderfully refreshing salad for a hot summer's day. Try it with the optional goat cheese to make a substantial meal — goat cheese goes remarkably well with melon.

INGREDIENTS

1lb (450g) spaghettini

5½oz (150g) goat cheese, cut into small dice (optional)

FOR THE SALSA

1lb (450g) ripe but firm plum tomatoes, diced

½ cantaloupe, seeded and diced

2 tbsp pitted black olives, diced

½ garlic clove, crushed

¼ tsp crushed red pepper flakes

⅔ cup (150ml) extra virgin olive oil

salt and freshly ground pepper

1 For the salsa, place the diced tomatoes, melon, and olives in a bowl. Add the garlic, red pepper flakes, and olive oil, season with salt and pepper, toss well to combine, and marinate for 1 hour.

2 Cook the spaghettini in boiling, salted water according to package instructions until al dente. Drain well, place in a large serving bowl, add the salsa, then toss well to combine. Scatter the diced goat cheese on top, if desired, and serve.

Preparation & cooking time
25 minutes, plus 1 hour marinating time

Serves 4

Nutritional notes
calories 835; protein 19g; carbohydrates 92g; total fat 46g, of which saturated fat 10g; fiber 6g; sodium 587mg

SPINACH & CUMIN RAVIOLI WITH LEMON BUTTER

Cumin seeds add an unexpected, pleasant, spicy note to a classic filling of spinach and ricotta for these homemade ravioli.

INGREDIENTS

1 batch basic pasta dough (see page 43)
1 tbsp olive oil
FOR THE FILLING
2 tbsp (25g) butter
1 garlic clove, crushed
1 tsp cumin seeds
½lb (250g) spinach, chopped
½ cup (100g) ricotta
1 tbsp freshly grated Parmesan
salt and freshly ground pepper
freshly grated nutmeg
FOR THE LEMON BUTTER
12 tbsp (175g) unsalted butter
½ garlic clove, crushed
½ cup (100ml) Vegetable Stock (see page 44)
zest and juice of 1 lemon, plus extra zest, to garnish
1 tbsp chopped fresh flat-leaf parsley, plus leaves, to garnish

1 For the filling, heat the butter in a pan with the garlic and cumin seeds. When the butter is frothy and the spices are fragrant, add the spinach and cook over low heat for 3–4 minutes, until tender. Transfer the mixture to a bowl, cover, and chill thoroughly.

2 When chilled, add the ricotta and Parmesan and stir until well combined. Season with salt, pepper, and nutmeg.

3 Roll out the pasta dough into four sheets (see page 43) and make and cook the ravioli (see steps 1–3, below).

4 When the ravioli are cooked and drained, place on a clean dish towel and pat off any excess moisture. Place the ravioli on a warmed plate, drizzle with olive oil, and keep warm while you prepare the lemon butter.

5 For the lemon butter, melt the butter with the garlic in a small pan over medium heat, add the stock, and bring to a boil. Reduce the heat to low and simmer for 5–8 minutes. Add the lemon zest and juice, stir, and season to taste.

6 Divide the ravioli among four serving plates. Pour a little lemon butter over the ravioli and serve garnished with a few strands of lemon zest, a sprinkling of chopped parsley, and a few parsley leaves.

Preparation & cooking time
1 hour, plus 1 hour for the stock, and 30 minutes for the pasta dough

Serves 4

Nutritional notes
calories 740; protein 18g; carbohydrates 49g; total fat 54g, of which saturated fat 31g; fiber 3g; sodium 343mg

MAKING & COOKING THE RAVIOLI

1 Lay out the pasta sheets on a lightly floured work surface. Brush the pasta with water, then put small teaspoons of filling onto the pasta in rows, placing them about 2 inches (5cm) apart.

2 Cover with a second sheet of pasta and cut into squares with a pasta wheel or sharp knife. Press the edges together with your fingers to ensure that they are well sealed. Place on a floured baking sheet.

3 Cook the ravioli in a pot of boiling, salted water. Cook for 2–3 minutes, then, when they rise to the surface, lift them out and drain on a slotted spoon.

PENNE WITH BROCCOLI & FAVA BEAN PESTO

It might seem fussy peeling the fava beans to make this pesto, but using only the tender inner kernel results in extra vibrancy of color and sweetness of flavor. This is a very fresh-tasting pesto, perfect for early summer.

INGREDIENTS

1lb (450g) broccoli, cut into small florets
1lb (450g) penne
salt and freshly ground pepper
freshly ground nutmeg
½ pint (150g) ripe cherry tomatoes, halved

FOR THE PESTO

¾lb (350g) fava beans, shelled
2 cups (50g) fresh basil, plus a few leaves, to garnish
1 tbsp pine nuts
2 tbsp freshly grated Parmesan, plus shavings, to garnish
2 garlic cloves, peeled
½ cup (100ml) extra virgin olive oil

1 For the pesto, blanch the fava beans in boiling water for 1 minute, refresh in cold water, then drain and dry them.

2 Peel off the outer skins to reveal the green beans. Place the beans in a blender or food processor with all the pesto ingredients, except the oil, and blend until finely chopped. With the motor still running, slowly drizzle in the oil until smooth and slightly runny. Season.

3 Blanch the broccoli in boiling, salted water for 3 minutes. Refresh in cold water; set aside.

4 Cook the penne in boiling, salted water according to package instructions until al dente; drain. Return to the pot, season with salt, pepper, and nutmeg, and mix in the broccoli and tomatoes. Transfer to a serving dish and add the pesto. Toss lightly and garnish with basil and Parmesan shavings.

Preparation & cooking time
30 minutes

Serves 4

Nutritional notes
calories 767; protein 27g; carbohydrates 96g; total fat 33g, of which saturated fat 6g; fiber 12g; sodium 181mg

---

LINGUINE WITH PORTOBELLO MUSHROOMS

Juicy, grilled mushrooms make a deeply flavorful sauce for pasta. Here, their flavor is intensified with a little red wine vinegar. You do not need to serve Parmesan cheese with this dish, so it is a good choice for vegans, too.

INGREDIENTS

9oz (250g) Portobello mushrooms
6 tbsp extra virgin olive oil
1lb (450g) linguine
1 tbsp red wine vinegar
2 tbsp chopped fresh mixed herbs (such as oregano, chives, mint, and thyme)
1 garlic clove, crushed
juice of ½ lemon
salt and freshly ground pepper

1 Trim the stems from the mushrooms and discard. Wipe the mushrooms with a cloth to remove any dirt.

2 Brush both sides of the mushrooms liberally with half the olive oil. Grill the mushrooms, preferably in a grill pan, or under a hot broiler, for 5–8 minutes, turning them occasionally, until tender.

3 Meanwhile, cook the linguine in boiling, salted water according to package instructions until al dente. Drain, then put back in the pot to keep warm. Toss in a little oil to prevent the pasta from sticking.

4 Remove the mushrooms from the pan and cut them into ¼ inch (5mm) slices. Put the mushrooms and any mushroom juices in a small bowl. Add the vinegar, remaining oil, herbs, garlic, and lemon juice to the mushrooms, mix together well, and season to taste.

5 Place the mushrooms in the pot with the pasta and toss together well. Serve in warmed, large, individual bowls.

Preparation & cooking time
30 minutes

Serves 4

Nutritional notes
calories 592; protein 16g; carbohydrates 94g; total fat 19g, of which saturated fat 2g; fiber 5g; sodium 114mg

CAPELLINI WITH ZUCCHINI & SAFFRON

The zucchini in this sauce are stewed with classic Provençal ingredients, such as olive oil, saffron, fennel seeds, and garlic, to make a delicate, summery sauce. Be sure to use the best, fresh, firm zucchini.

INGREDIENTS

4 large zucchini, cut in half lengthwise

6 tbsp olive oil

3 garlic cloves, crushed

½ tsp fennel seeds

good pinch of saffron or ¼ tsp powdered saffron

¾ cup (200g) canned crushed tomatoes

salt and freshly ground pepper

pinch of granulated sugar

1 lb (450g) capellini or other long, thin pasta

handful of fresh basil, chopped, to serve

1 Scoop out the center seeds from the zucchini with a teaspoon, then cut the zucchini into ¼ inch (5mm) thick slices to form small crescents.

2 Heat the oil in a skillet, add the garlic, fennel seeds, and saffron, and cook over medium heat for 30 seconds. Add the zucchini and stir well to coat with the oil.

3 Reduce the heat and let the zucchini stew for 12–15 minutes, until it is soft and translucent. Add the tomatoes and cook for 5 minutes. Season with salt and pepper and stir in the sugar.

4 Cook the pasta in boiling, salted water according to package instructions until al dente. Drain, then toss in the vegetables. Adjust the seasoning and serve sprinkled with fresh basil.

Preparation & cooking time
45 minutes

Serves 4

Nutritional notes
calories 569; protein 16g; carbohydrates 89g; total fat 19g, of which saturated fat 3g; fiber 5g; sodium 123mg

SPAGHETTI WITH FENNEL, CHARD & PARMESAN

This simple sauce of lightly caramelized vegetables works well with a variety of pasta shapes, but here I have used it with spaghetti. You could also serve the vegetables on their own.

INGREDIENTS

1 fennel, with fronds

4 tbsp olive oil

1 onion, thinly sliced

¾ lb (300g) Swiss chard, washed and roughly shredded

1 cup (75g) sun-dried tomatoes

4 tbsp balsamic vinegar

½ cup (100ml) Vegetable Stock (see page 44)

1 lb (450g) spaghetti

¾ cup (100g) freshly grated Parmesan

salt and freshly ground pepper

freshly grated nutmeg

1 Remove the fronds from the fennel and thinly slice it. Reserve the fennel and fronds.

2 Heat half the oil in a large skillet, add the onion and fennel, and sauté over medium heat for 8–10 minutes, until golden and soft.

3 Add the chard and sweat for 2–3 minutes longer until the chard just begins to wilt. Stir in the sun-dried tomatoes and balsamic vinegar.

4 Pour in the vegetable stock, raise the heat, and bring to a boil. Reduce the heat and simmer until the stock has evaporated and the chard is tender. Meanwhile, cook the spaghetti in boiling, salted water according to package instructions until al dente. Drain, return to the pot, and keep warm.

5 When the chard is tender, add the cooked spaghetti to the pan with half the Parmesan. Toss lightly together and season with salt, pepper, and nutmeg.

6 Transfer to a serving bowl, scatter the fennel fronds on top, sprinkle with the remaining oil and Parmesan, and serve.

Preparation & cooking time
45 minutes, plus 1 hour for the stock

Serves 4

Nutritional notes
calories 734; protein 27g; carbohydrates 92g; total fat 31g, of which saturated fat 8g; fiber 6g; sodium 734mg

RED PEPPER TAGLIATELLE WITH CHILI SAUCE

This spicy, homemade tagliatelle is surprisingly easy to make. Blended in a food processor and then rolled out using a hand-cranked pasta machine, it can be ready to go in the pot within just half an hour of beginning the preparations.

INGREDIENTS

FOR THE PASTA DOUGH

2 red peppers, halved and seeded

1 small red chili, seeded and chopped

2 large eggs, plus 1 large egg yolk

1 tbsp olive oil

3¾ cups (425g) unbleached flour, plus extra, to dust

1 tsp salt

FOR THE SAUCE

⅔ cup (150ml) olive oil

2 garlic cloves, crushed

½ tsp red chili oil

2 zucchini, sliced

1 red pepper, halved, seeded, and quartered

2 small eggplants, sliced

1 red onion, cut into thin rings

6 oyster mushrooms

salt and freshly ground pepper

1 For the pasta dough, blend the peppers to a coarse puree in a blender or food processor. Add the chili and blend. Add the eggs and oil and blend until smooth. Mix in the flour and salt until you have a firm dough. Cover and let rest for 30 minutes.

2 Knead the dough, roll it out into thin sheets, and cut into thin strips (see page 43).

3 For the sauce, mix together the olive oil, crushed garlic, chili oil, and salt in a large bowl. Toss the vegetables in the mixture to coat them. Remove the vegetables from the oil and reserve the oil. Broil the vegetables on a high setting for 5 minutes on each side, until golden and tender. Return the vegetables to the oil.

4 Cook the tagliatelle in a pot of boiling, salted water for 2 minutes, until al dente. Drain the pasta, then toss with the vegetables and oil, and season.

Preparation & cooking time
40 minutes, plus 30 minutes resting time

Serves 4

Nutritional notes
calories 897; protein 20g; carbohydrates 102g; total fat 49g, of which saturated fat 8g; fiber 8g; sodium 666mg

ASIAN POTSTICKERS

If you do not have the time to make the dough for this recipe, you can always buy a package of wonton wrappers measuring 3 inches (7cm) square and use them instead. Serve with your favorite dipping sauce.

INGREDIENTS

1¼ cups (150g) all-purpose flour, plus extra, to dust

½ cup (110ml) boiling water

2 tbsp soy sauce

Chinese Dipping Sauce (see page 52) or a Thai sweet chili sauce, to serve

FOR THE FILLING

4 tbsp vegetable oil

½ onion, finely chopped

1 inch (2.5cm) piece of fresh ginger, finely chopped

1 garlic clove, crushed

¼ tsp crushed red pepper flakes

¼lb (150g) shiitake mushrooms, chopped

⅓ cup (75g) dried black beans, soaked overnight and cooked (see page 41)

¾ cup (50g) bread crumbs

2 tbsp chopped fresh cilantro

salt and freshly ground pepper

1 For the dough, place the flour in a large bowl. Gradually stir in the water until most of it is incorporated; add more water if the dough is too dry. Knead for 5–6 minutes, until smooth. Return the dough to the bowl, cover with plastic wrap, and let rest in a cool place for 30 minutes.

2 For the filling, heat half the oil in a skillet and cook the onion, ginger, garlic, and pepper flakes for 1 minute over medium heat. Raise the heat, add the mushrooms and beans, and cook for 4 minutes. Add the bread crumbs and cilantro, mix well, season, then let cool.

3 Knead the dough with a little more flour. Roll into ropes 8 inches (20cm) long by ¾ inch (2cm) wide. Cut into 20 equal segments. Roll each one into 2½ inch (6cm) flat rounds. Place on a lightly floured baking sheet.

4 Place 1 tablespoon of the filling in the center of each round of dough. Moisten the edge with water and pinch together with your fingers to seal and form small half-moons.

5 Heat the remaining oil in a large, nonstick pan until hot. Place the potstickers in the pan in one layer and cook them over medium heat until they are lightly browned on one side.

6 Add ⅔ cup (150ml) water and the soy sauce and cover. Raise the heat a little and cook for 10–12 minutes, until the liquid is absorbed and the potstickers are crisp on one side.

7 Arrange the potstickers on a plate, crisp side up. Serve with the Chinese dipping sauce or a Thai sweet chili sauce.

Preparation & cooking time
2¼–2¾ hours, plus overnight soaking time

Serves 4

Nutritional notes
calories 392; protein 13g; carbohydrates 56g; total fat 14g, of which saturated fat 2g; fiber 3g; sodium 925mg

BAKED SWEET POTATO GNOCCHI WITH LEMON

Make sure that you buy the orange-fleshed sweet potatoes rather than the white ones to make these unusual gnocchi — not only is the color more attractive but the flavor is sweeter, too.

INGREDIENTS

1lb (450g) orange sweet potatoes

½ cup (50g) freshly grated Parmesan, plus 2 tbsp extra, to serve

2 tbsp (25g) butter

2 egg yolks

1¼ cups (150g) all-purpose flour, plus extra, to dust

good pinch of cinnamon

salt and freshly ground pepper

pinch of freshly grated nutmeg

FOR THE SAUCE

½ cup (125ml) Vegetable Stock (see page 44)

9 tbsp (125g) butter

2 tbsp chopped fresh cilantro

zest and juice of ½ lemon

1 Bake the sweet potatoes whole for 1–1¼ hours, until tender. When cool enough, peel, then mash them in a bowl while they are still warm. Add the Parmesan, butter, egg yolks, and half the flour. Add the cinnamon, seasoning, and nutmeg.

2 Turn the mixture onto a floured surface and knead in the remaining flour, a little at a time, to form a smooth dough. Roll into ¾ inch (2cm) thick ropes, then cut into ½ inch (1cm) lengths. Place on a floured baking sheet and let dry for 1 hour.

3 Poach the gnocchi, a few at a time, in a pot of boiling, salted water for 4–5 minutes. When they rise to the surface, remove with a slotted spoon and drain. Season with salt, pepper, and nutmeg and keep warm.

4 For the sauce, boil the stock and butter together, add the cilantro and lemon zest and juice, and season. Arrange the gnocchi in a serving bowl and pour the sauce over them. Serve with Parmesan.

Oven preheated to
400°F/200°C

Preparation & cooking time
2½ hours, plus
1 hour for the stock

Serves 4

Nutritional notes
calories 612; protein 14g;
carbohydrates 53g;
total fat 40g, of which
saturated fat 25g;
fiber 4g; sodium 622mg

OLIVE BREAD GNOCCHI

These are one of the easiest gnocchi to make and the bread crumbs give them a lovely light texture. They can be served with just a sprinkling of cheese, or with a tomato or red pepper sauce (see right) for a more substantial dish.

INGREDIENTS

1lb (450g) olive bread, made into bread crumbs

1½ cups (350ml) milk

1 egg, beaten

1 cup (125g) freshly grated Parmesan

1 tsp salt

4 cups (450g) flour, plus extra, to dust

FOR THE SAUCE

7 tbsp (100g) butter, plus extra, to grease

1 garlic clove, crushed

2 tbsp chopped fresh basil

1 Place the bread crumbs in a bowl, then add the milk, egg, Parmesan, and salt. Add enough flour to make a thick dough and knead for 4–5 minutes, until pliable. Turn out onto a floured work surface and knead until soft.

2 Roll the dough into 1 inch (2.5cm) thick ropes. Cut the ropes into ¾ inch (2cm) pieces. Roll each piece individually and place on a floured baking sheet.

3 Drop the gnocchi, a few at a time, into a pot of boiling, salted water. Reduce the heat, then simmer for 2–3 minutes. When they rise to the surface, remove with a slotted spoon and place in a buttered serving dish.

4 For the sauce, heat the butter in a skillet until foaming. Add the garlic and basil, then pour the sauce over the gnocchi.

Preparation & cooking time
25 minutes

Serves 4

Nutritional notes
calories 1103; protein 40g;
carbohydrates 152g;
total fat 42g, of which
saturated fat 24g;
fiber 9g; sodium 2555mg

TRICOLOR GNOCCHI WITH PEPPER SAUCE

Appropriately enough, these red, green, and white gnocchi share the colors of the Italian flag. Ricotta cheese makes them nice and light, while a warm red pepper and tomato vinaigrette replaces the usual butter and cheese sauces.

INGREDIENTS

1 cup (250g) ricotta, drained
1¾ cups (200g) freshly grated Parmesan
¾ cup (100g) all-purpose flour, plus extra, to dust
1 egg, plus 1 egg yolk, beaten together
½ lb (200g) fresh spinach, stalks removed
1 tbsp sun-dried tomato (or tomato) paste
salt and freshly ground pepper
pinch of freshly grated nutmeg

FOR THE SAUCE

1 red pepper, halved and seeded
⅔ cup (150ml) olive oil
1 garlic clove, crushed
pinch of granulated sugar
4 tomatoes, peeled, seeded, and chopped (see page 39)
bunch of fresh basil, chopped, plus leaves, to garnish

1 Mix together the cheeses, flour, and eggs until well combined; season. Divide into three and place each portion in a separate bowl. Cover and chill for 1 hour.

2 Cook the spinach in its own water over medium heat for 2 minutes, until tender. Drain well, then finely chop. Add the spinach to one bowl of cheese mixture, the sun-dried tomato paste to the second, and leave the third plain. Season all three with salt, pepper, and nutmeg and mix well.

3 With floured hands, roll each mixture into 1 inch (2.5cm) balls. Toss the balls in flour and set on a floured baking sheet. Cook in a pot of boiling, salted water for 3–5 minutes, until they rise to the surface. Remove with a slotted spoon and keep warm.

4 For the sauce, blend the red pepper in a blender or food processor until smooth, then strain. Heat the pepper in a pan over low heat with the olive oil, garlic, and sugar for 5 minutes. Add the tomatoes and basil and cook for 1 minute; season to taste.

5 Divide the gnocchi among four bowls, making sure each has an equal amount of red, green, and white gnocchi. Coat with the warm pepper sauce and serve garnished with sprigs of fresh basil leaves.

Preparation & cooking time
1½ hours

Serves 4

Nutritional notes
calories 848; protein 33g; carbohydrates 28g; total fat 67g, of which saturated fat 21g; fiber 3g; sodium 860mg

STEWS & STIR-FRIES

These warming stews, stir-fries, casseroles, and curries are perfect for chilly days. A diverse range of ingredients is used in the recipes, and they often include rich sauces or wholesome toppings. They are simple to prepare and are therefore ideal both for entertaining and for more casual meals with friends. Some are robust dishes, cooked slowly to maximize the fragrances and flavors of various ingredients; others are lighter fare, simply sautéed or stir-fried to seal in the flavors.

ROOT VEGETABLE PIE WITH POLENTA CRUST

KEY INGREDIENTS

Small white onions are full of flavor and lend texture and taste

Passata, pure, sieved tomatoes, comes in a waxed box

Polenta is finely ground golden cornmeal, used often in Italian cooking

Baby carrots, Jerusalem artichokes, baby parsnips, and baby turnips provide contrasting colors and textures

Cannellini beans are good, all-purpose beans that are deliciously soft when cooked

On a cold winter's day, what could be more welcome than a warming root vegetable casserole? This one is cooked in a rich red wine and tomato sauce, and then baked with a golden polenta topping to make a satisfying pie. The polenta crust also makes an interesting topping for baked pasta dishes.

INGREDIENTS

1lb (400g) selection mixed root vegetables (such as baby carrots, Jerusalem artichokes, baby parsnips, baby turnips, and rutabaga)

6 tbsp olive oil

1 onion, chopped

1 garlic clove, crushed

¼lb (150g) small white onions, peeled

¼lb (150g) chestnut mushrooms, sliced

15oz (425g) can cannellini beans, drained

⅔ cup (150ml) full-bodied red wine

2½ cups (600ml) Dark Vegetable Stock (see page 44)

2½ cups (600ml) tomato passata

salt and freshly ground pepper

FOR THE TOPPING

2 eggs

¾ cup (175ml) plain yogurt

1¼ cups (150g) grated Cheddar

¾ cup (100g) instant polenta

¾ cup (100g) all-purpose flour

1 tsp baking powder

1 Peel and dice the root vegetables, but only scrub the baby vegetables. Heat the oil in a large pan and cook the onion and garlic over medium heat for 5 minutes, until golden and soft. Add all the vegetables, the white onions, and mushrooms and cook them over medium heat, stirring all the time, for 8 minutes, until golden and slightly softened.

2 Add the beans, wine, stock, and passata. Bring to a boil, season, then transfer to a deep, 9 inch (23cm) ovenproof dish and bake for 20–25 minutes.

3 Meanwhile, for the topping, whisk the eggs and yogurt together in a bowl. Stir in half the cheese, all the polenta, flour, and baking powder and mix well. Remove the dish from the oven and spread the topping over it to make a thick crust. Sprinkle the remaining cheese over the top and bake for 25 minutes, until golden.

Oven preheated to
375°F/190°C

Preparation & cooking time
1½ hours, plus 1 hour for the stock

Serves 4

Nutritional notes
calories 771; protein 31g; carbohydrates 77g; total fat 37g, of which saturated fat 12g; fiber 11g; sodium 963mg

WINTER VEGETABLE ROOTATOUILLE

Ratatouille is one of those classic dishes that is usually regarded as sacred, but I like to experiment, and I was delighted to find that ingredients with traditional Provençal flavors, such as garlic, olives, oregano, and tomatoes, make a perfect match for root vegetables.

INGREDIENTS

6 tbsp olive oil
½ lb (250g) red potatoes, peeled and cut into 1 inch (2.5cm) wedges
½ lb (250g) parsnips, sliced
½ lb (250g) rutabaga, cut into 1 inch (2.5cm) wedges
1 cup (150g) carrots, sliced
2 garlic cloves, crushed
½ cup (50g) pitted black olives
¾ cup (200g) canned tomatoes, drained and chopped
⅔ cup (150ml) tomato passata
2 tsp chopped fresh oregano, or 1 tsp dried oregano
salt and freshly ground pepper

1 In a large casserole dish, heat the olive oil and sauté the root vegetables and garlic together for 2–3 minutes over medium heat, stirring occasionally.

2 Add the olives and cook for 5 minutes longer, then add the tomatoes and passata.

3 Cover the dish and transfer to the oven. Bake for 50 minutes, until the vegetables are just cooked and coated in the sauce. Check the casserole from time to time and add a little water or stock if it becomes too dry. Add the oregano 5 minutes before the end of the cooking time, season, and stir.

Oven preheated to 375°F/190°C

Preparation & cooking time 1¼ hours

Serves 4

Nutritional notes calories 295; protein 4g; carbohydrates 28g; total fat 19g, of which saturated fat 3g; fiber 7g; sodium 427mg

ULTIMATE SHEPHERD'S PIE WITH MASHED POTATO

A pie, I am sure, that any shepherd would be proud of! What makes it special is its luxurious topping of buttery, mashed new potatoes with scallions and parsley. Root vegetables in a light sauce are a delicious alternative to the traditional meat filling normally associated with this dish.

INGREDIENTS

¼ lb (150g) parsnips, cut into 1 inch (2.5cm) pieces
¼ lb (150g) celeriac, cut into 1 inch (2.5cm) pieces
2 carrots, cut into 1 inch (2.5cm) pieces
1 sweet potato, cut into 1 inch (2.5cm) pieces
¼ lb (150g) Jerusalem artichoke, cut into 1 inch (2.5cm) pieces
¼ lb (150g) pearl onions
4½ cups (1 liter) Vegetable Stock (see page 44)
3 tbsp (50g) butter, plus extra, to grease
2 tbsp all-purpose flour
1¼ cups (300ml) milk
salt and freshly ground pepper
1 tbsp Dijon mustard
FOR THE TOPPING
2lb (900g) waxy potatoes, washed and cut into equal-size pieces
5 tbsp (75g) unsalted butter
4 scallions, finely chopped
2 tbsp roughly chopped fresh flat-leaf parsley

1 For the topping, cook the potatoes in boiling, salted water for 20–25 minutes, until tender. Drain, then mash them roughly with a fork. Add half the butter, the scallions, and parsley. Season and mix well.

2 For the pie, simmer the vegetables in the stock for 15 minutes, until tender. Drain, reserving 1¼ cups (300ml) stock, and keep the vegetables warm.

3 Heat the butter in a medium pan over medium heat. Stir in the flour, then slowly add the milk. Heat until it boils and thickens. Reduce the heat and cook for 8–10 minutes. Add the reserved stock, season, and add the mustard. Mix in the vegetables.

4 Spoon the mixture into a greased, ovenproof dish and cover with the topping. Dot with the remaining butter. Bake for 20–25 minutes, until piping hot and brown and crispy on top.

Oven preheated to 400°F/200°C

Preparation & cooking time 1¾ hours, plus 1 hour for the stock

Serves 6

Nutritional notes calories 403; protein 8g; carbohydrates 50g; total fat 20g, of which saturated fat 13g; fiber 7g; sodium 268mg

ASIAN STIR-FRY WITH COCONUT & LEMONGRASS

The refreshing citrus taste of lemongrass adds a delicate Asian note to any dish. This simple stir-fry is enriched with coconut milk and ketjap manis, an Indonesian, aniseed-flavored, sweet soy sauce. Serve it with fragrant Thai white rice.

INGREDIENTS

10½oz (300g) broccoli, cut into florets
1 ear of corn, cut into 8 pieces
1 inch (2.5cm) piece of fresh ginger
3 tbsp (50g) butter
2 tbsp sesame oil
1 garlic clove, crushed
¼ tsp turmeric
2 stalks lemongrass, finely shredded
2 green chilies, seeded and thinly sliced
¼lb (75g) sugar-snap peas
½ cup (50g) bean sprouts
2 carrots, sliced
2 scallions, sliced
¼lb (75g) oyster or shiitake mushrooms
1¾ cups (400ml) canned coconut milk
2 tbsp ketjap manis (Indonesian soy sauce)
¼lb (125g) firm tofu, cubed (optional)
salt and freshly ground pepper
cilantro leaves, to garnish

1 Blanch the broccoli and corn on the cob for 5 minutes in separate pots of boiling water. Drain and set aside.

2 Finely chop the ginger. Heat the butter and sesame oil in a wok or deep-sided skillet. When hot, add the garlic, ginger, and turmeric and cook together for 30 seconds to release the fragrances into the oil.

3 Add the shredded lemongrass and the chilies, then stir in all the vegetables. Stir-fry for 4–5 minutes, until the vegetables are cooked but still crisp. Add the coconut milk, ketjap manis, and tofu, if using.

4 Stir to combine, then bring to a boil. Boil for 2 minutes, then adjust the seasoning to taste. Garnish with cilantro leaves.

Preparation & cooking time
30 minutes

Serves 4

Nutritional notes
calories 392; protein 21g; carbohydrates 25g; total fat 25g, of which saturated fat 8g; fiber 4g; sodium 770mg

CAULIFLOWER & LENTIL PALAK

Lentils and cauliflower are both sadly misused in vegetarian cooking and are often overcooked and underseasoned. In India, these two simple ingredients are treated with respect. Combined with an aromatic spice paste and cooked gently, they make a fragrant and satisfying dish. Serve this palak with basmati rice.

INGREDIENTS

1 inch (2.5cm) piece of fresh ginger, peeled
2 garlic cloves, peeled
2 green chilies, seeded
1 onion, chopped
½ cup (125ml) plain yogurt
6 tbsp vegetable oil
4 cardamom pods, cracked
1 bay leaf
1 tsp ground cumin
¼ tsp turmeric
1 tsp ground coriander
1 large cauliflower, cut into florets
1 cup (200g) brown lentils, cooked (see page 41)
¾ cup (200g) canned crushed tomatoes
1¼ cups (300ml) Vegetable Stock (see page 44)
½lb (200g) fresh or frozen spinach
salt and freshly ground pepper

1 Puree the ginger, garlic, and chilies in a blender or food processor. Stir in half the onion and all the yogurt; set aside.

2 Heat half the oil in a large pan. Add the cardamom and bay leaf and cook over low heat for 30 seconds. Add the remaining onion and cook until lightly browned. Add the cumin, turmeric, and ground coriander. Cook for 10–12 minutes longer.

3 Add the cauliflower, lentils, and yogurt mixture, then the tomatoes, remaining oil, and stock. Cook over low heat, stirring gently, for 10–12 minutes, until the cauliflower is tender and the sauce has reduced. Chop the spinach and add 5 minutes before the end of cooking. Season before serving.

Preparation & cooking time
1 hour 10 minutes, plus 1 hour for the stock

Serves 4

Nutritional notes
calories 400; protein 21g; carbohydrates 36g; total fat 20g, of which saturated fat 3g; fiber 8g; sodium 232mg

PAUL'S RATATOUILLE NICOISE

Everybody knows and loves ratatouille, so what is different about mine? Heating the basil and oil together and adding them to the ratatouille at the end of the cooking time brings a freshness and vitality that I know you will enjoy.

INGREDIENTS

4 tbsp extra virgin olive oil	vegetable oil
1 onion, finely chopped	1 large eggplant, cut into ¾ inch (2cm) dice
4 garlic cloves, crushed	2 red peppers, halved, seeded, and cut into ¾ inch (2cm) dice
½ tbsp tomato paste	1 green pepper, halved, seeded, and cut into ¾ inch (2cm) dice
1½lb (650g) ripe tomatoes, peeled, seeded (see page 39), and quartered	¾lb (350g) zucchini, cut into ¾ inch (2cm) slices
½ tsp superfine sugar	12 fresh basil leaves, chopped
1 bouquet garni, made up of celery, leek, rosemary, thyme, ½ bay leaf, oregano, and basil (see page 39)	salt and freshly ground pepper

Oven preheated to 375°F/190°C

Preparation & cooking time 1¼ hours

Serves 4

Nutritional notes
calories 307; protein 5g; carbohydrates 19g; total fat 24g, of which saturated fat 3g; fiber 7g; sodium 128mg

1 Heat 2 tablespoons of the olive oil in a heavy-bottomed pan, add the onion and half the garlic, and sweat over medium heat for 5 minutes, until soft. Stir in the tomato paste, reduce the heat, and cook for 2–3 minutes. Stir in the tomatoes and sugar and add the bouquet garni. Cook over low heat for 10–15 minutes, stirring, until thickened.

2 In a large skillet, heat 4 tablespoons of vegetable oil. Cook the eggplant over medium heat for 5–10 minutes, stirring occasionally until golden. Add more oil if needed. Drain.

3 Heat a little more vegetable oil in the same pan and add the peppers. Cook over low heat for 8–10 minutes, stirring, until tender, then drain. Finally, add a little more oil to the pan and cook the zucchini for about 2 minutes on either side until tender and golden. Drain in the colander.

4 Add the vegetables to the tomato mixture. Season lightly and transfer to a large, ovenproof dish. Cover and bake for 10–15 minutes.

5 Heat the remaining olive oil in a small pan with the remaining garlic and the basil and cook for a few seconds until the basil is wilted. Remove the ratatouille from the oven. Discard the bouquet garni, then stir in the garlic and basil oil. Adjust the seasoning and serve hot.

PUMPKIN, SWEET POTATO & BANANA CURRY

Although many vegetables would work well in this curry, I particularly like the contrast between the sweet vegetables, the banana, and the fiery sauce. The refreshing yogurt and cilantro chutney takes seconds to prepare and makes a good accompaniment to other hot curries and spicy dishes. Serve this dish with the rice of your choice.

INGREDIENTS

2 tbsp vegetable oil
1 onion, finely chopped
1 garlic clove, crushed
1 inch (2.5cm) piece of fresh ginger, finely grated
½ tsp fenugreek seeds
1 stalk lemongrass, finely chopped
4 tbsp Thai red curry paste
½ tsp turmeric
¾ lb (350g) pumpkin, peeled, seeded, and cut into large cubes
¾ lb (300g) sweet potato, peeled and cut into large cubes
1¼ cups (300ml) Vegetable Stock (see page 44)
1¼ cups (300ml) coconut milk
salt and freshly ground pepper
2 bananas, peeled and diced

FOR THE YOGURT CHUTNEY

⅔ cup (150ml) plain yogurt
½ tsp mustard seeds
2 tbsp chopped fresh cilantro, plus a few leaves, to garnish

1 Heat the oil in a large pan and cook the onion, garlic, ginger, and fenugreek over low heat for about 5 minutes, until the onion is softened. Stir in the lemongrass, curry paste, and turmeric.

2 Add the pumpkin and sweet potato and stir to coat them in the spices. Cook over low heat for 2–3 minutes to allow the vegetables to absorb the flavors of the spices.

3 Pour in the vegetable stock and coconut milk. Bring to a boil, lower the heat, and simmer gently for 15–20 minutes, until the vegetables are tender. Season, remove from the heat, and then add the diced bananas.

4 For the chutney, blend together all the ingredients in a blender or food processor. When the curry is cooked, garnish it with a few fresh cilantro leaves. Serve it with the yogurt chutney on the side.

Preparation & cooking time
50 minutes, plus 1 hour for the stock

Serves 4

Nutritional notes
calories 285; protein 6g; carbohydrates 41g; total fat 12g, of which saturated fat 2g; fiber 4g; sodium 549mg

WILD MUSHROOM STROGANOFF WITH SPATZELE

Spatzele, which means "little sparrows" in German, are tiny, dumpling-like noodles, a specialty of Alsace and Germany. They are convenient because they can be poached a day or two in advance, then stored in the refrigerator and heated in butter at the last moment. Here, spinach-flavored spatzele are served in elegant little mounds to accompany a rich, Russian-inspired mushroom stew.

INGREDIENTS

2 tbsp olive oil
1 tbsp Hungarian paprika
1¼lb (550g) mixed wild mushrooms, well cleaned
2 shallots, finely chopped
3 tbsp white wine vinegar
6 tbsp dry white wine
1¼ cups (300ml) heavy cream
⅔ cup (150ml) Brown Mushroom Stock (see page 44)
1 tbsp cocktail gherkins, thinly shredded
1 tsp Dijon mustard

FOR THE SPATZELE

¼lb (150g) spinach, blanched and finely chopped
5 eggs, lightly beaten
3 cups (350g) all-purpose flour
¼ tsp baking powder
salt and freshly ground pepper
freshly grated nutmeg
3 tbsp (50g) butter

1 For the spatzele, blend together the spinach, eggs, and ½ cup (125ml) water in a blender or food processor. Sift the flour into a bowl, add the baking powder, and season with salt, pepper, and nutmeg. Add the spinach mixture.

2 See steps 1–3 below for how to make the spatzele. When cooked, refresh in ice water. Use immediately, or toss in oil and keep in the refrigerator until needed.

3 For the stroganoff, heat the oil in a skillet. Place half the paprika on a large plate and dredge the mushrooms in it, then sprinkle them with salt. Cook the seasoned mushrooms over medium heat for 1 minute. Add the shallots and cook for another minute. Lift out the mushrooms and keep warm.

4 Pour the vinegar and wine into the pan containing the shallots and bring to a boil. Stir in the cream and reduce the sauce by half. Add the stock, then reduce the sauce until thick enough to coat the back of a spoon. Add the gherkins and stir in the mustard and remaining paprika. Stir in the mushrooms and season.

5 Heat the butter in a large pan and cook the spatzele for 2 minutes, until golden. Season with salt, pepper, and nutmeg, then place in dariole molds. Turn the spatzele out onto serving plates. Serve hot with the stroganoff.

Preparation & cooking time
1 hour,
plus 1 hour for the stock

Serves 4

Nutritional notes
calories 953; protein 24g; carbohydrates 75g; total fat 63g, of which saturated fat 33g; fiber 6g; sodium 553mg

MAKING THE SPATZELE

1 Gently beat together the ingredients (see step 1, above) to form a smooth, very thick batter, almost like dough in texture.

2 Place a colander over a pot of boiling, salted water. Pour a third of the batter in at a time. Press the batter through the holes with a spatula.

3 When the spatzele float to the surface, reduce the heat. Cook for 3–4 minutes, until they swell and become fluffy. Remove with a slotted spoon.

HUNGARIAN STEW WITH CARAWAY DUMPLINGS

Hungarian cuisine is full of hearty stews, spiced with pungent, sweet paprika and topped with light, fluffy dumplings. This combination works well for vegetarians too, especially now that vegetarian suet is so easy to obtain. You can steam the dumplings on top of the casserole for the last ten minutes of cooking instead of poaching them, if you prefer.

INGREDIENTS

4 tbsp olive oil

1 garlic clove, crushed

¼lb (100g) small white onions

1 celery stalk, sliced

1 carrot, sliced

½ rutabaga, cut into large dice

1 kohlrabi, cut into large dice

1 medium parsnip, sliced

½ medium cauliflower, cut into florets

1 potato, cut into large dice

1 tsp caraway seeds

1 tbsp Hungarian paprika

1 tbsp tomato paste

2 tbsp all-purpose flour

1¼ cups (300ml) white wine

2½ cups (600ml) Vegetable Stock (see page 44)

salt and freshly ground pepper

3 tbsp chopped fresh parsley, to garnish

FOR THE DUMPLINGS

½ cup (50g) rye flour

½ cup (50g) self-rising flour

1½oz (40g) vegetarian suet

pinch of caraway seeds

1 tsp grated fresh horseradish

1 Heat the olive oil in a large, heavy-bottomed pan and cook the garlic, onions, and celery over medium heat for 4–5 minutes, until golden. Add the remaining vegetables and cook for 2 minutes, until browned, then add the caraway seeds, paprika, and tomato paste. Cook for 3 minutes longer.

2 Add the flour and cook, stirring, for 2–3 minutes. Gradually pour in the wine and stock, stirring. Season and bring to a boil. Lower the heat and simmer for 15–20 minutes, until tender.

3 For the dumplings, place the flours in a bowl with a little salt and pepper. Stir in the suet, caraway seeds, and horseradish. Add 4 tablespoons of water, or enough to bind the mixture into a smooth, firm dough. Roll the dough into 12 separate 1 inch (2.5cm) balls.

4 Poach the dumplings in a pan of boiling, salted water for 10 minutes, until light and fluffy. Place on the casserole to serve and sprinkle with the parsley.

Preparation & cooking time
1 hour 10 minutes, plus 1 hour for the stock

Serves 4

Nutritional notes
calories 501; protein 10g; carbohydrates 58g; total fat 22g, of which saturated fat 6g; fiber 9g; sodium 202mg

PINTO BEAN, EGGPLANT & TAHINI MOUSSAKA

For me, eggplant and sesame have a great affinity. In this recipe for a rich, vegetarian version of this Greek dish, I infuse a classic white sauce with tahini, a sesame seed paste: it gives a wonderful, characteristic nutty flavor.

INGREDIENTS

1 cup (150g) dried pinto beans, soaked overnight and cooked (see page 41)
6 tbsp vegetable oil
1 onion, chopped
1 garlic clove, crushed
½ tsp ground cumin
2 tsp chopped fresh thyme, or 1 tsp dried thyme
¾ cup (200g) canned crushed tomatoes
1 tbsp tomato paste
2 large eggplants, sliced
salt and freshly ground pepper

FOR THE SAUCE

2 garlic cloves, peeled, but left whole
1¼ cups (300ml) milk
2 tbsp (25g) butter
¼ cup (25g) flour
1 tbsp tahini (sesame seed paste)
1 egg, beaten

1 For the sauce, place the garlic cloves in a small pan with the milk. Cook over low heat for about 20 minutes, until the garlic is very soft. Blend the milk and garlic in a blender; set aside.

2 For the moussaka, drain the pinto beans, reserving any cooking liquid. Heat 2 tablespoons of the oil in a large pan and sweat the onion and garlic over medium heat for 5 minutes, until golden. Add the cooked pinto beans, cumin, thyme, crushed tomatoes, and tomato paste. Stir in the reserved cooking liquid from the beans and simmer for 20–25 minutes, until the sauce has thickened. Season.

3 Heat the remaining oil in a large skillet and cook the eggplant over medium heat for 5 minutes on each side until golden. Remove and drain the excess oil on paper towels.

4 Arrange a layer of eggplant in the bottom of an ovenproof dish. Cover it with half the pinto beans, then another layer of eggplant, the remaining beans, and a final layer of eggplant.

5 For the sauce, melt the butter in a small pan, stir in the flour to make a roux, and cook for 1 minute. Gradually stir in the garlic-infused milk and bring to a boil, stirring until the sauce thickens. Stir in the tahini paste and beat in the egg. Cook for 2–3 more minutes, stirring. Season to taste.

6 Spoon the sauce over the eggplant, to cover. Bake for 30–35 minutes, until the topping is golden and bubbling.

Oven preheated to 400°F/200°C

Preparation & cooking time 1½ hours, plus overnight soaking time

Serves 4

Nutritional notes calories 445; protein 15g; carbohydrates 37g; total fat 28g, of which saturated fat 8g; fiber 10g; sodium 259mg

RICE & GRAINS

RICE AND GRAINS have traditionally provided the staple diets for people all around the world, and they are particularly important sources of nutrients for vegetarians. This section includes recipes that are traditional favorites in countries as far apart as Italy and Indonesia. I have included timeless classics such as paella and risotto and given them a new twist by fusing Eastern and Western flavors. I have also combined rice and grains with legumes to produce dishes that are packed with goodness.

MARDI GRAS JAMBALAYA

KEY INGREDIENTS

Thyme and bay leaves combine to impart a subtle flavor to stews

Celery, green pepper, and onion provide an excellent base for many stews, stocks, and sauces because they all have such strong flavors

Okra and baby corn are typical ingredients in Creole cooking

Arborio rice is the Italian risotto rice, but it can be used in any dish that calls for rice with a creamy texture

Red kidney beans are full of protein and bring a splash of color to many dishes

This all-vegetable version of Louisiana's dazzling, famous Creole rice dish captures the color and excitement of the New Orleans great, annual Mardi Gras festival.

INGREDIENTS

3 tbsp sunflower or olive oil
2 celery stalks, thinly sliced
1 green pepper, diced
1 onion, chopped
2 garlic cloves, crushed
1 large bay leaf
2 sprigs fresh thyme
4½ cups (1 liter) Vegetable Stock (see page 44)
¼ lb (150g) fresh okra
1½ cups (425g) canned crushed tomatoes
½ cup (100g) baby corn
¼ lb (150g) peeled squash or pumpkin, cut into ¾ inch (2cm) cubes
1½ cups (250g) arborio rice
salt and freshly ground pepper
pinch of cayenne
15oz (425g) can red kidney beans, washed and drained
2 tbsp chopped fresh parsley

1 Heat a large, heavy-bottomed pan over medium heat. Add the oil and cook the celery, pepper, onion, and garlic for 7 minutes, until lightly browned. Add the bay leaf and thyme and cook for 2 minutes longer. Add the stock, stir well, and bring to a boil.

2 Meanwhile, trim off the tops of the okra stems. Add the okra, tomatoes, baby corn, and squash to the pan, reduce the heat, and simmer for 5 minutes. Then stir in the rice.

3 Season with salt, pepper, and cayenne, to taste. Bring back to a boil, then reduce the heat to low and simmer gently for 20 minutes, stirring occasionally.

4 Stir in the beans and parsley, and cook for 5 minutes more. When the rice is done, check the seasoning. Serve hot.

🕐 **Preparation & cooking time**
55 minutes, plus 1 hour for the stock

◎ **Serves 4**

♡ **Nutritional notes**
calories 455; protein 14g; carbohydrates 79g; total fat 12g, of which saturated fat 2g; fiber 9g; sodium 443mg

NASI GORENG

Perfect for a quick, satisfying snack, this spicy, Indonesian fried rice dish can be served with whatever garnishes you have on hand. Try cucumber, roasted peanuts, or chopped, fresh cilantro. You can buy plum sauce from most supermarkets these days.

INGREDIENTS

FOR THE CHILI SAMBAL

4 tbsp vegetable oil

2 inch (5cm) piece of fresh ginger, grated

4 tomatoes, chopped

2 red chilies, seeded and chopped

FOR THE RICE

4 tbsp vegetable oil

1 onion, finely chopped

1 garlic clove, crushed

¼lb (100g) white cabbage, finely shredded

1 cup (200g) long-grain rice, boiled

1 red chili, seeded and shredded

½ cup (50g) cooked peas

2 tbsp ketjap manis (Indonesian soy sauce)

4 eggs

TO SERVE

1 banana, sliced

4 scallions, sliced

plum sauce

1 For the chili sambal, blend together all the ingredients in a blender or food processor to form a smooth paste.

2 For the rice, heat the oil in a wok over medium heat. Add the onion and garlic and cook for 5 minutes. Add the cabbage and stir-fry for 1–2 minutes. Stir in the chili sambal and mix well.

3 Continue to stir-fry for 1 minute. Increase the heat and add the cooked rice and chili. Stir-fry for 2–3 minutes to heat the rice through. Stir in the peas and ketjap manis and heat for a minute longer. Keep warm.

4 Fry the eggs. Pile the rice on four serving plates, top with the banana, and set 1 egg on each portion. Garnish with the scallions. Spoon the plum sauce around to serve.

Preparation & cooking time
50 minutes

Serves 4

Nutritional notes
calories 518; protein 7g; carbohydrates 71g; total fat 25g, of which saturated fat 3g; fiber 3g; sodium 457mg

THAI-INSPIRED RISOTTO WITH PUMPKIN

This is one of the most successful East-West hybrids I have come across. It combines the classic Italian method of cooking risotto with fragrant Thai flavorings, such as lemongrass, coconut milk, and cilantro. In keeping with the Asian theme, the cooked risotto is sprinkled with grated coconut instead of Parmesan.

INGREDIENTS

3 tbsp (40g) butter
1 onion, chopped
1 garlic clove, crushed
1 lemongrass stalk, thinly sliced
1 red chili, seeded and chopped
½ tsp curry powder
1 inch (2.5cm) piece of fresh ginger, chopped
¾lb (350g) pumpkin, peeled and cut into ½ inch (1cm) pieces
1¾ cups (350g) arborio rice
½ cup (100ml) dry white wine
3¼ cups (700ml) Vegetable Stock (see page 44)
⅔ cup (150ml) coconut milk
1 tbsp chopped fresh mint
1 tbsp chopped fresh cilantro
salt and freshly ground pepper
grated coconut, to serve

1 Melt the butter in a large, heavy-bottomed pan. Add the onion, garlic, lemongrass, chili, curry powder, and ginger, and cook, stirring, over low heat for 5 minutes. Add the pumpkin and rice and cook for 1 minute more. Pour in the wine and a ladleful of stock and cook, stirring, until the liquid is absorbed.

2 Keep adding the stock, a ladleful at a time, stirring constantly, until the rice is tender but al dente, about 25 minutes. Toward the end of cooking, add the stock in smaller quantities and check frequently to see if the rice is cooked.

3 Add the coconut milk, mint, and cilantro. Remove from the heat, season, and sprinkle with grated coconut to serve.

Preparation & cooking time
50 minutes, plus 1 hour for the stock

Serves 4

Nutritional notes
calories 448; protein 8g; carbohydrates 83g; total fat 12g, of which saturated fat 6g; fiber 2g; sodium 223mg

COCONUT RICE WITH ALMONDS & RAISINS

The rice in this dish gets its vivid color from plenty of ground turmeric, which also adds a subtle flavor. It makes an attractive and tasty accompaniment to Indian and other Asian dishes.

INGREDIENTS

1½ cups (350ml) Vegetable Stock (see page 44)
1¼ cups (300ml) coconut milk
2 tbsp turmeric, mixed to a paste with 2 tbsp cold water
1 lemongrass stalk, braised (see page 40)
2 cups (350g) long-grain rice
TO SERVE
2 tbsp toasted, slivered almonds
1 green chili, seeded and very thinly sliced
2 tbsp raisins, soaked in cold water overnight

1 Combine the vegetable stock and coconut milk in a pan and bring to a boil, then reduce the heat to low and simmer. Stir in the turmeric paste, lemongrass, and rice, and stir well. Cover and simmer for 15 minutes, until all the water has been absorbed. Remove from the heat and leave, covered, for 2–3 minutes. Discard the lemongrass.

2 Transfer to a serving dish and sprinkle the almonds, chili, and raisins over the top to serve.

Preparation & cooking time
30 minutes, plus 1 hour for the stock, plus overnight soaking for the raisins

Serves 4

Nutritional notes
calories 440; protein 9g; carbohydrates 90g; total fat 8g, of which saturated fat 1g; fiber 1g; sodium 98mg

VEGETARIAN PAELLA

In Spain, paella is cooked outdoors, over a wood fire. In less sunny climates you might have to abandon authenticity and retreat indoors to prepare this dish. The important thing is to use a good olive oil, genuine saffron, and short-grain rice. If you cannot get Spanish rice, use arborio rice instead.

INGREDIENTS

⅔ cup (150ml) Vegetable Stock (see page 44), plus more if needed

½ tsp saffron

½ cup (50g) peas

1 tbsp olive oil

1 onion, finely chopped

2 garlic cloves, crushed

2 Jerusalem artichokes, diced

1 eggplant, diced

3 peppers (1 red, 1 yellow, 1 green), halved, seeded, and chopped

2 celery stalks, sliced

1 tsp Spanish paprika

2 tbsp (50g) Spanish short-grain rice

6 tbsp dry white wine

1½ cups (425g) canned crushed tomatoes

½ cup (50g) green beans, cooked

2 tbsp pitted black olives

flat-leaf parsley, to garnish

lemon wedges, to serve

1 Put ⅔ cup (150ml) vegetable stock and the saffron in a large pot and bring to a boil, then remove from the heat and set aside. In a separate pot, boil the peas for about 5 minutes, until tender.

2 Heat the oil in a large pan and cook the onion and garlic for 5 minutes over medium heat, until golden. Add the artichokes, eggplant, peppers, celery, paprika, and rice and stir to coat in the oil. Cook for 2–3 minutes, stirring occasionally, until the rice becomes transparent.

3 Pour in the white wine and saffron-infused stock. Stir in the chopped tomatoes, reduce the heat, and cook for 20 minutes, until tender. Add more stock if the rice becomes too dry. Stir in the green beans, olives, and peas. Garnish with parsley and place the lemon wedges on the side.

Preparation & cooking time
1 hour,
plus 1 hour
for the stock

Serves 4

Nutritional notes
calories 199; protein 6g; carbohydrates 32g; total fat 5g, of which saturated fat 1g; fiber 8g; sodium 130mg

LEMON COUSCOUS & CHERMOULA MUSHROOMS

The Moroccan spice mix "chermoula" gives the mushrooms a tantalizing aroma as they cook. Lemon pepper — finely ground dried lemon zest — is a useful ingredient for flavoring grains and other bland foods. I first experienced lemon pepper on my travels in the Caribbean.

INGREDIENTS

3 tbsp vegetable oil

1 onion, chopped

2 garlic cloves, crushed

1 tsp cumin seeds

½ tsp crushed red pepper flakes

½ lb (200g) chestnut mushrooms, halved

6 portobello mushrooms, thickly sliced

1 tsp harissa paste

1½ cups (425g) canned crushed tomatoes

2 tbsp finely chopped fresh cilantro

FOR THE COUSCOUS

1¼ cups (200g) couscous

1¼ cups (250ml) Vegetable Stock (see page 44), boiling

juice of ½ lemon

1 tbsp Lemon Pepper (see page 45)

salt and freshly ground pepper

1 Place the couscous in a bowl with the vegetable stock and lemon juice and cover. Leave for 5 minutes, until the couscous has swollen. Fluff it up with a fork, cover again, and leave for 5 more minutes. Add the lemon pepper, season to taste with salt and pepper, and keep warm.

2 Heat the oil in a pan and cook the onion and garlic over medium heat for 5 minutes. Add the cumin and red pepper flakes and cook for a few seconds. Add the mushrooms and harissa. Cook for 3 minutes, then add the tomatoes. Bring to a boil, reduce the heat, and simmer for 8–10 minutes. Stir in the cilantro. Serve the lemon couscous topped with the mushroom mixture.

Preparation & cooking time
30 minutes,
plus 1 hour
for the stock

Serves 4

Nutritional notes
calories 237; protein 7g; carbohydrates 33g; total fat 10g, of which saturated fat 1g; fiber 2g; sodium 162mg

TOASTED MILLET & CUMIN VEGETABLES

I like to use millet rather than the more familiar couscous in this recipe. Its wonderful nutty flavor and crunchy texture make it a good partner for the roasted root vegetables. You can, of course, substitute couscous if you prefer. I sometimes top the vegetables with a little firm, diced goat cheese for a tasty variation.

INGREDIENTS

4 small parsnips, halved lengthwise

4 carrots, halved lengthwise

8 new potatoes, quartered

1 sweet potato, cut lengthwise into wedges

1 leek, cut into ½ inch (1cm) slices

4 very small beets, boiled and halved

FOR THE MARINADE

1 cup (200ml) olive oil

2 bay leaves

2 garlic cloves, crushed

2 tbsp balsamic vinegar

1 tbsp ground cumin

¼ cup (50g) raisins, soaked overnight

4 tbsp chopped fresh cilantro, plus leaves, to garnish

FOR THE MILLET

1½ cups (275g) millet

1 garlic clove, crushed

¼ tsp ground cumin

2½ cups (600ml) Vegetable Stock (see page 44)

salt and freshly ground pepper

1 Combine all the vegetables, except the beets, in a large bowl and add all the marinade ingredients. Toss the vegetables and marinade ingredients together well and marinate for 1 hour.

2 Arrange the vegetables with the beets in a single layer in a shallow roasting pan. Roast for 25–30 minutes, until lightly browned. Reduce the heat to 325°F/170°C, cover the pan, and cook for 30 minutes longer until the vegetables are firm outside, but soft inside.

3 Toast the millet in a large nonstick skillet over medium heat for about 5 minutes. Add the garlic and cumin. Meanwhile, bring the stock to a boil in a separate pot, then add the millet. Season lightly and cover. Reduce the heat and simmer for about 25 minutes, until all the liquid has evaporated and the millet is tender and fluffy.

4 To serve, arrange a mound of millet on each serving plate, pile the roasted vegetables on top, and pour the roasting juices left in the pan over the vegetables. Garnish with cilantro.

Oven preheated to
425°F/220°C

Preparation & cooking time
2 hours, plus 1 hour for the stock, plus 1 hour marinating time, plus overnight soaking for the raisins

Serves 4

Nutritional notes
calories 990; protein 11g; carbohydrates 118g; total fat 54g, of which saturated fat 8g; fiber 12g; sodium 233mg

SUCCOTASH PUDDING

Succotash is a traditional Native American dish made with corn and beans. This baked version contains a double dose of corn — corn kernels and cornmeal — plus red peppers and tomatoes for a colorful, savory pudding.

INGREDIENTS

9 tbsp (125g) butter, plus extra, to grease

1 onion, finely chopped

1 garlic clove, crushed

1¼ cups (200g) frozen or canned corn

3 tomatoes, peeled, seeded, and chopped (see page 39)

1 red pepper, halved, seeded, and diced

¾ cup (75g) green or fava beans, cooked

¼ tsp paprika

½ cup (75g) cornmeal

salt and freshly ground pepper

1 Heat 2 tbsp (25g) of the butter in a pan, add the onion and garlic, and sweat for 5 minutes over medium heat, until soft. Transfer to a bowl and add all the remaining ingredients, except the cornmeal and remaining butter. Mix well, add the cornmeal, and season.

2 Butter a shallow, 5 cup (1.2 liter) casserole dish. Melt the remaining butter over low heat and pour it over the cornmeal mixture. Mix again. Spoon into the casserole, and bake for 1 hour, until puffed and golden.

Oven preheated to
325°F/160°C

Preparation & cooking time
1½ hours

Serves 4

Nutritional notes
calories 254; protein 6g; carbohydrates 36g; total fat 10g, of which saturated fat 6g; fiber 4g; sodium 317mg

POLENTA VERDE WITH WILD MUSHROOMS

This green polenta gets its color from the Savoy cabbage, but you could use fresh spinach instead. The polenta squares or rounds can be prepared well in advance and kept in the refrigerator for up to two days, then baked just before serving.

INGREDIENTS

FOR THE POLENTA

3 tbsp (50g) butter, plus extra, to grease, and to brush

1 garlic clove, crushed

½ Savoy cabbage, shredded

¾ cup (85g) quick-cooking polenta

¼ cup (25g) freshly grated Parmesan

½ tsp chopped fresh thyme

1 egg yolk, beaten

½ cup (50g) finely grated fontina

salt and freshly ground pepper

FOR THE MUSHROOMS

3 tbsp (50g) butter

¼ lb (100g) mixed mushrooms

1 tbsp balsamic vinegar

2 tbsp chopped fresh chives, to garnish

1 Melt the butter in a large pan, add the garlic and cabbage, and cook over low heat for 12–15 minutes, stirring all the time, until the cabbage is soft.

2 Bring 3¼ cups (700ml) of water to a boil and cook the polenta (see step 1, below). When the polenta is cooked, remove from the heat, stir in the cabbage mixture, then add the

Parmesan, thyme, and egg yolk and stir well. Let the polenta set (see step 2, below).

3 Cover the polenta with plastic wrap and place in the refrigerator for at least 4 hours, or preferably overnight, until set and firm to the touch. When set, turn out and cut (see step 3, below).

4 Lightly grease a baking sheet and transfer the portions of polenta to the sheet. Brush the polenta with melted butter and sprinkle with the fontina. Bake for 25–30 minutes, until golden and sizzling.

5 Meanwhile, for the mushrooms, heat the butter in a large skillet and sauté the mushrooms over high heat for 5–8 minutes, until cooked. Season, then add the balsamic vinegar. Cook for 2–3 minutes more, still over high heat, stirring gently.

6 To serve, place a portion of polenta on each of six serving dishes, top with a mound of the mushrooms, and garnish with chopped chives.

 Oven preheated to 400°F/200°C

Preparation & cooking time
1¼ hours, plus 4 hours or overnight to set

Serves 6

Nutritional notes
calories 248; protein 8g; carbohydrates 12g; total fat 19g, of which saturated fat 12g; fiber 2g; sodium 325mg

PREPARING THE POLENTA

1 Add the polenta to the pan of boiling, salted water, stirring constantly. Season and cook over medium heat, stirring all the time, for 8–10 minutes, until smooth and thick.

2 Transfer the mixture to a shallow baking sheet lined with plastic wrap and spread it out evenly with a narrow spatula, pressing down lightly as you spread.

3 Turn the chilled polenta out onto a clean work surface. Cut out six 4 inch (10cm) squares with a knife, or six 3¾–4 inch (9–10cm) rounds with a pastry cutter.

STUFFED VEGETABLES

THESE RECIPES DEMONSTRATE how to add an extra dimension to vegetables as varied as the humble potato, the versatile pepper, and the more unusual gem squash. Nature has provided many vegetables complete with the perfect cooking vessel: their own shells. Stuffed vegetables not only look spectacular; the stuffings also retain their flavor and moisture when they are encased in succulent roast flesh. Small, stuffed vegetables make pretty appetizers, while larger ones, or larger servings, make ideal main dishes.

GREEK BABY VEGETABLES WITH ORZO

KEY INGREDIENTS

Mushrooms are full of flavor and texture

Orzo, a tiny pasta shaped like barley, is perfect for stuffings

Eggplant, zucchini, and red pepper are widely used in Greek cooking

Raisins are sweet and combine perfectly with salty feta

Mint has a fresh, light flavor

Feta is a soft, fresh Greek cheese with a sharp, tangy taste

Stuffed vegetables are frequently offered as part of a meze (selection of snacks) in Greece, but a large selection of mixed, stuffed vegetables makes a splendid main course. You can serve them hot, but the Greek way is to serve them at room temperature. Orzo is a rice-shaped pasta, but rice would work equally well in the filling.

INGREDIENTS

4 tomatoes, halved
4 baby peppers
4 baby eggplants
4 small zucchini
4 mushrooms, stems removed
½ cup (125ml) vegetable oil
salt and freshly ground pepper

FOR THE STUFFING

¼lb (115g) feta, diced
½ cup (100g) orzo pasta, cooked
½ tbsp ground cumin
½ tbsp ground coriander
1½ tbsp raisins, soaked in water
1½ tbsp peanuts, toasted
1 tbsp chopped fresh mint
½ small onion, chopped

FOR THE SAUCE

½ cup (100ml) extra virgin olive oil
½ tbsp chopped fresh flat-leaf parsley
1 tbsp chopped fresh oregano
2 garlic cloves, crushed
juice of 1 lemon

1 Slice off the tomato tops and discard. Scoop out the seeds. Cut the tops off the peppers and seed them. Reserve the tops. Place all the vegetables except the tomatoes on the baking sheet with the pepper tops and brush with oil. Season and roast for 15 minutes; let cool.

2 Cut a small, horizontal slice off the top of each eggplant and zucchini, and scoop out the center. Mix half the feta with the other stuffing ingredients and the scooped out flesh from the vegetables. Fill all the vegetables with this mixture.

3 Place the vegetables and the tomatoes on the baking sheet, season, then bake for 5 minutes.

4 Blend together the sauce ingredients and 6 tablespoons of water. Replace the pepper tops. Place the vegetables on a plate, scatter the remaining feta around, and drizzle with the sauce.

Oven preheated to 400°F/200°C

Preparation & cooking time 45 minutes, plus 2 hours soaking time

Serves 4

Nutritional notes calories 712; protein 10g; carbohydrates 23g; total fat 66g, of which saturated fat 12g; fiber 6g; sodium 535mg

SQUASH WITH TOFU

1 Bring a large pot of lightly salted water to a boil and blanch the squash whole for 10 minutes, until tender. Drain them and set aside.

2 Heat the oil in a skillet, add the garlic and sun-dried tomatoes, and cook on medium heat for 5 minutes, until softened, but not browned. Transfer to a bowl, then add the olives, bread crumbs, egg, thyme leaves, and tofu. Stir until well combined with the garlic and tomatoes. Season to taste, then let cool.

3 Slice the top from each squash and carefully scoop out the seeds with a metal spoon; discard the seeds. Fill each squash with the tofu and thyme stuffing.

4 Turn the broiler onto low heat. Place the squash under the broiler (without the tops) to cook slowly for 25–30 minutes until tender and heated through. Serve hot, with or without the tops, garnished with sprigs of fresh thyme on top.

Preparation & cooking time
1 hour

Serves 4

Nutritional notes
calories 221; protein 8g; carbohydrates 27g; total fat 10g, of which saturated fat 2g; fiber 4g; sodium 427mg

Tofu is often dismissed as bland and boring, but the great thing about it is that it absorbs the flavors of other ingredients — here an Italian-inspired mixture of sun-dried tomatoes, black olives, and thyme. Gem squash are perfect for single servings, but you could use two butternut squash, halved, instead.

INGREDIENTS

4 gem or 2 butternut squash
1 tbsp olive oil
1 garlic clove, crushed
½ cup (25g) sun-dried tomatoes
½ cup (25g) pitted black olives, chopped
1 cup (50g) fresh bread crumbs
1 egg, beaten
2 tsp fresh thyme leaves, plus fresh thyme sprigs, to garnish
¼lb (100g) firm tofu, cubed
salt and freshly ground pepper

TOMATOES WITH GOAT CHEESE PESTO

Try to get well-flavored, firm, ripe tomatoes for this dish. You could use cherry tomatoes and serve them as canapés, but preparing them will require time and patience.

INGREDIENTS

4 medium tomatoes
¼lb (125g) mozzarella, grated
5½oz (150g) soft goat cheese
4 tbsp pesto
salt and freshly ground pepper
4 tbsp olive oil
6 tbsp Vinaigrette (see page 45)
handful of fresh basil leaves, to garnish

1 Cut the tomatoes in half and scoop the seeds into a bowl. Put the seeds in a sieve and strain; reserve the resulting juice. Place the tomatoes upside down on a plate for 5 minutes to drain. Add the juice that collects on the plate to the reserved juice.

2 In a bowl, mix together the cheeses, tomato juice, and pesto. Season, then fill each tomato half with the mixture. Brush the tomatoes with the olive oil and place them on a baking tray under a hot broiler. Broil for about 5 minutes, until golden.

3 Place the tomatoes on a large serving plate and drizzle with a little vinaigrette. Garnish each tomato with a basil leaf.

Preparation & cooking time
30 minutes

Serves 4

Nutritional notes
calories 446; protein 11g; carbohydrates 4g; total fat 43g, of which saturated fat 11g; fiber 1g; sodium 437mg

SAVOY CABBAGE WITH CELERIAC & CHESTNUTS

Chestnuts always remind me of Christmas and, with a rich, velvety Madeira sauce, this makes an ideal festive dish. The ramekins can be filled a few hours or a day in advance, then kept in the refrigerator and cooked just before serving.

INGREDIENTS

1 small Savoy cabbage
5 tbsp (75g) butter
½ celeriac, peeled and cut into ½ inch (1cm) dice
1 onion, finely chopped
1 garlic clove, crushed
¼lb (100g) mushrooms, diced
4½oz (125g) can chestnuts, drained and chopped or 2oz (50g) dried chestnuts, reconstituted
6 tbsp heavy cream
1 small egg, beaten
3 tbsp vegetable suet, grated
salt and freshly ground pepper
freshly grated nutmeg

FOR THE TARRAGON SAUCE

2 tbsp (25g) unsalted butter
¾ cup (75g) mushrooms, thinly sliced
3 tomatoes, peeled, seeded, and chopped (see page 39)
1 tbsp chopped fresh tarragon
⅔ cup (150ml) Madeira Sauce (see page 44)

1 Prepare the cabbage leaves (see step 1, below) and shred the remaining cabbage as finely as possible with a sharp knife.

2 Heat half the butter and cook the celeriac for 5–8 minutes over medium heat until golden. Add 2 tablespoons of water, cover, and braise for 15 minutes, until the celeriac is tender and the liquid has evaporated.

3 Sauté the onion, garlic, mushrooms, and chestnuts in the remaining butter over medium heat for 5 minutes. Add the shredded cabbage and cream, and cook over low heat for 10 minutes, until the vegetables are tender and the sauce thickened.

4 Transfer to a bowl and, when cool, mix in the egg, suet, and celeriac. Season with salt, pepper, and nutmeg. Stuff the cabbage leaves (see steps 2–3, below). Place the ramekins in a roasting pan. Pour in boiling water to come one third of the way up the sides of the ramekins. Bake for 40 minutes.

5 For the sauce, heat the butter and fry the mushrooms for 3 minutes over medium heat. Add the tomatoes and tarragon, and cook for 1 minute. Stir in the Madeira sauce and cook for 5 minutes over low heat. Turn out the packages. Serve with the sauce.

Oven preheated to 400°F/200°C

Preparation & cooking time 1 hour 45 minutes, plus 1 hour for the Madeira Sauce

Serves 4

Nutritional notes calories 438; protein 5g; carbohydrates 16g; total fat 39g, of which saturated fat 23g; fiber 5g; sodium 254mg

STUFFING THE CABBAGE

1 Remove eight outer cabbage leaves. Cut out the center rib of each one and discard. Blanch the leaves in boiling water for 2 minutes.

2 Line each of four 3¼ inch (8cm) ramekins with a cabbage leaf, leaving no gaps, so that the leaf hangs over the sides. Spoon in the filling.

3 Place another leaf over the filling, tuck in over the filling, and bring the overhanging bottom leaf over the top. Press down lightly to seal.

ASIAN STUFFED EGGPLANTS

Eggplants stuffed with Mediterranean ingredients have become a popular vegetarian dish, but I find that Asian flavors work equally well and make an interesting change. If you would like a spicier version, simply add more finely chopped chili and a little more ginger and cilantro.

INGREDIENTS

4 medium eggplants

6 tbsp peanut oil

1 onion, chopped

2 garlic cloves, crushed

1 red chili, finely chopped

1 inch (2.5cm) piece of fresh ginger, chopped

1 tbsp coriander seeds

¼lb (150g) fresh spinach

8 water chestnuts, peeled and sliced

¾ cup (150g) canned chopped tomatoes

2 tbsp chopped fresh cilantro, plus fresh cilantro leaves, to garnish

1 tsp black sesame seeds

FOR THE SAUCE

⅔ cup (150ml) Vegetable Stock (see page 44)

2 tbsp tamari or light soy sauce

½ tsp superfine sugar

1 tbsp dry sherry

2 tbsp lemon juice

2 tsp cornstarch, mixed to a paste with 1 tbsp cold water

salt and freshly ground pepper

Oven preheated to 350°F/180°C

Preparation & cooking time 1 hour 45 minutes, plus 1 hour for the stock

Serves 4

Nutritional notes calories 251; protein 5g; carbohydrates 16g; total fat 19g, of which saturated fat 4g; fiber 6g; sodium 712mg

1 Cut a lid from the top of each eggplant and reserve, then remove a thin slice from each base. Set the eggplants on a greased baking sheet, brush them all over with 2 tablespoons of oil, and bake for 30–35 minutes. When cool, scoop out the flesh, leaving a ½ inch (1cm) shell. Chop the flesh.

2 Heat the remaining oil in a pan and cook the onion, garlic, chili, ginger, and coriander seeds over a low heat for 5–8 minutes, until the onions are tender. Stir in the spinach and chestnuts, raise the heat a little, and cook for 2 minutes.

3 Add the tomatoes to the pan with the fresh cilantro. Simmer for 15–20 minutes. Mix in the eggplant flesh and season.

4 Stuff the eggplant shells with the mixture, place them on the baking sheet, with the lids on the side, and bake for 15–20 minutes.

5 For the sauce, bring the stock, tamari, sugar, sherry, and lemon juice to a boil. Lower the heat to a simmer, add the cornstarch paste, and stir until thickened. Surround the eggplants with the sauce and sprinkle with the sesame seeds. Garnish with cilantro.

STUFFED ROASTED ONIONS

Onions are a basic ingredient in so many dishes, but they deserve to play a starring role, too. Roasted onions taste sweet and tender, combining well with this mushroom and cheese filling. You could serve them with a Fresh Tomato Sauce (see page 45).

INGREDIENTS

4 large onions, unpeeled
4 tbsp peanut or vegetable oil
1 garlic clove, crushed
¼lb (150g) chestnut mushrooms, diced or 2oz (50g) selection of dried, wild mushrooms, soaked for 30 minutes, drained
1 tbsp fresh thyme leaves
1 tbsp chopped fresh parsley
¼ cup (25g) Cheddar, grated
2 tbsp freshly grated Parmesan
¾ cup (50g) fresh white bread crumbs
salt and freshly ground pepper

1 Cook the onions in salted, boiling water for 8–10 minutes. Cool under cold running water for a few seconds, then pat dry.

2 Carefully peel off the outer skins, then, using a sharp knife, cut the top off each onion and reserve. Carefully scoop out the flesh, leaving two or three outer layers of onion.

3 Finely chop the onion flesh. Heat half the oil in a skillet, and cook the chopped onion and garlic over low heat for about 5 minutes, until soft. Add the mushrooms and herbs and cook for 4–5 minutes longer.

4 Remove from the heat and let cool slightly. Mix in the Cheddar and season to taste. Fill the onion shells with the mixture. Mix together the Parmesan and bread crumbs, and sprinkle over the top.

5 Pour the remaining oil on top, and bake the onions on a baking sheet, with the tops on the side, for 20–25 minutes. Serve hot, with or without the tops.

Oven preheated to 400°F/200°C

Preparation & cooking time 1–1¼ hours, plus 30 minutes soaking time

Serves 4

Nutritional notes calories 270; protein 8g; carbohydrates 26g; total fat 16g, of which saturated fat 5g; fiber 4g; sodium 269mg

ITALIAN BAKED MUSHROOMS

Because the stuffing needs no precooking, this is very quick to prepare. The stuffing is lighter than the usual bread crumb-based stuffings, so the mushrooms make an ideal appetizer.

INGREDIENTS

8 large mushrooms
½ small onion, chopped
1 cup (75g) sun-dried tomatoes, chopped
¼ cup (100g) spinach, cooked
3oz (75g) mozzarella, diced
2 garlic cloves, crushed
½ tbsp chopped fresh parsley
1 tbsp chopped fresh basil
6 tbsp extra virgin olive oil, plus extra, to grease
salt and freshly ground pepper

FOR THE DRESSING

1 red chili, seeded and finely diced
8 fresh basil leaves, roughly chopped
3 tbsp (50g) pine nuts
½ cup (125ml) olive oil
2 tbsp balsamic vinegar
1½ cups (100g) sun-dried tomatoes, chopped

1 Remove the stems from the mushrooms. Set the mushroom cups aside until the filling is ready, and dice the stems roughly.

2 Place the diced mushroom stems in a bowl with the onion, tomatoes, spinach, mozzarella, garlic, parsley, basil, and olive oil. Toss together and season well.

3 Fill the mushroom cups with the mixture, then place on a lightly oiled baking sheet. Bake for 10–15 minutes, until the cups are tender and the cheese in the stuffing has melted.

4 For the dressing, blend all the ingredients together. Place two mushrooms on each plate and drizzle with the dressing.

Oven preheated to 325°F/160°C

Preparation & cooking time 30 minutes

Serves 4

Nutritional notes calories 803; protein 10g; carbohydrates 4g; total fat 83g, of which saturated fat 13g; fiber 1g; sodium 585mg

POTATO BRANDADE WITH TRUFFLE OIL

These are essentially baked potatoes, but the most luxurious version imaginable. Baking potatoes are most suitable — this recipe will not work with waxy varieties. The truffle oil in the dressing is so pungent that just a small amount gives a remarkably heady scent and flavor.

INGREDIENTS

5 medium to large baking potatoes
2 garlic cloves, crushed
1 egg yolk
4 tbsp extra virgin olive oil
½ cup (50g) Parmesan shavings
salt and freshly ground pepper
8 fresh chives, to garnish

FOR THE DRESSING

1 tbsp white truffle oil
3 tbsp olive oil
1 tbsp balsamic vinegar
4 sun-dried tomatoes, chopped

1 Bake the potatoes for about 1 hour, until cooked through.

Halve the potatoes lengthwise and scoop the flesh into a bowl, leaving a ½ inch (1cm) shell. Discard two of the shells. Mix the garlic into the flesh and let cool a little before beating in the egg yolk. Drizzle in the olive oil, beating constantly; season.

2 Spoon the flesh back into the eight half shells. Place on a baking sheet and return to the oven for 2–3 minutes, to heat through. Blend together all the dressing ingredients and season. Top the potatoes with shavings of Parmesan, drizzle the dressing around or over the potatoes, and garnish with chives.

Oven preheated to 400°F/200°C

Preparation & cooking time 1 hour 25 minutes

Serves 4

Nutritional notes calories 556; protein 13g; carbohydrates 55g; total fat 33g, of which saturated fat 7g; fiber 4g; sodium 359mg

---

CARIBBEAN CHAYOTES

Members of the squash family, chayotes have a bland taste that combines well with spicy flavorings. They are very popular in Caribbean cooking, so I have given a Caribbean accent to the stuffing in this recipe, using coconut, chili, and curry powder.

INGREDIENTS

4 medium chayotes
2 tomatoes, peeled and seeded (see page 39)
4 tbsp clarified butter or vegetable oil
1 onion, chopped
1 garlic clove, crushed
4 cardamom seeds
½ tsp curry powder
1 green chili, seeded and finely chopped
¾ cup (125g) corn
2 tbsp chopped fresh cilantro
1 tbsp dried coconut

1 Boil the chayotes whole for 35 minutes, until tender. Halve lengthwise and scoop out the flesh, leaving a ½ inch (1cm) shell. Reserve the flesh. Chop the tomatoes finely.

2 Heat 2 tablespoons of the butter in a skillet. Cook the onion, garlic, cardamom, and curry powder over medium heat for 5 minutes, until soft. Mash the chayote pulp and add to the pan with the remaining ingredients. Heat through for 5 minutes.

3 Spoon the mixture into the chayote shells and drizzle the remaining butter over the top. Broil under medium heat or bake for 8–10 minutes, until golden. Serve hot.

Oven preheated to 400°F/200°C

Preparation & cooking time 1 hour 10 minutes

Serves 4

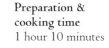

Nutritional notes calories 238; protein 5g; carbohydrates 31g; total fat 12g, of which saturated fat 7g; fiber 6g; sodium 100mg

RED PEPPERS WITH FENNEL & CORN

Whole red peppers make perfect containers for this rich, creamy filling. With their golden crust of Parmesan and cornmeal, they look quite stunning. I love the flavor of caraway seeds, which echoes the fennel, but they are not to everyone's taste, so omit them if you prefer.

INGREDIENTS

4 red peppers
2 tbsp olive oil, plus extra, to grease
salt and freshly ground pepper

FOR THE FILLING

2 small fennel, chopped
⅔ cup (150ml) heavy cream
2 garlic cloves, crushed
1 tsp caraway seeds
½ cup (100g) corn kernels
1 tbsp pine nuts, toasted
½ cup (55g) Parmesan, grated
2 tbsp cornmeal

1 Slice the tops off the peppers and set them aside. Seed the peppers. Brush the insides with oil and season. Put the peppers upright on an oiled baking sheet, and bake, with the tops on the side, for 12–15 minutes, until tender.

2 For the filling, blanch the fennel in boiling water for 2–3 minutes, until tender. Drain. Heat the cream with the garlic, caraway, and fennel over low heat. Cook gently for 15 minutes, until the sauce is thick. Add the corn and pine nuts. Season.

3 Fill the peppers with the fennel mixture. Mix together the Parmesan and the cornmeal and sprinkle over the peppers. Return to the oven for 5 minutes, until golden. Replace the tops and serve.

Oven preheated to 400°F/200°C

Preparation & cooking time 50–55 minutes

Serves 4

Nutritional notes calories 421; protein 11g; carbohydrates 23g; total fat 32g, of which saturated fat 15g; fiber 6g; sodium 281mg

GOLDEN PEPPERS WITH ZUCCHINI PEPERONATA

This is the sort of food we are all supposed to be eating more of: lots of fresh vegetables lightly cooked in a little olive oil. With the lively flavors of chili, capers, and olives, this recipe makes a great appetizer or light lunch dish.

INGREDIENTS

4 yellow peppers
2 tbsp olive oil, plus extra, to grease
salt and freshly ground pepper

FOR THE PEPERONATA

4 tbsp olive oil
1 onion, chopped
2 garlic cloves, crushed
½ tsp crushed red pepper flakes
¾lb (300g) baby zucchini, sliced
4 small tomatoes, halved
1 tbsp chopped fresh oregano
2 tbsp red wine vinegar
1 tbsp capers, rinsed and drained
1 tbsp pitted black olives, chopped

1 Slice the tops off the peppers and reserve the tops. Seed the peppers. Brush the insides with oil and season. Put the peppers upright on an oiled baking sheet, and bake, with the tops on, for 12–15 minutes, until the peppers are lightly charred and just tender.

2 For the peperonata, heat the olive oil in a large skillet, add the onion, and fry over low heat for 5 minutes, until soft. Add the garlic and red pepper flakes, and cook for 2 minutes longer.

3 Add the zucchini and sauté for 1 minute, still over low heat. Add the tomatoes, season, and cook gently, covered, for 8–10 minutes, until the tomatoes have softened and a sauce begins to form around the zucchini.

4 Remove the lid of the pan and add half the oregano. Stir well, then pour in the vinegar, and add the capers and olives. Adjust the seasoning, then fill the roasted peppers with the mixture. Return the peppers to the oven for 15 minutes longer, sprinkle with the reserved oregano, replace the tops, and serve.

Oven preheated to 400°F/200°C

Preparation & cooking time 50–55 minutes

Serves 4

Nutritional notes calories 234; protein 4g; carbohydrates 15g; total fat 18g, of which saturated fat 3g; fiber 5g; sodium 166mg

SALADS

THE FAMOUS 19TH-CENTURY gastronome Brillat Savarin once said of salad, "It freshens without enfeebling, and fortifies without irritating." Here is a selection of salads with a riot of tastes and textures that are also deliciously fortifying. There are substantial salads combining cheese, noodles, or bread with crisp vegetables, and salads with Asian, Middle Eastern, and Mediterranean influences. Some can be served as side dishes or appetizers, while others make spectacular main courses.

JAPANESE OMELETTE SALAD

KEY INGREDIENTS

Soy sauce is made from fermented soybeans and lends sweetness and depth

Snow peas are flat-podded peas that can be eaten whole

Glutinous or sushi rice is a short- to medium-grain rice, prized for its sticky texture

Yellow peppers add color to salads and are packed with vitamins

Cucumber is always a welcome addition to salads with its cool, refreshing taste

Watercress has a wonderful peppery flavor and is rich in iron and calcium

Packed full of goodness, this salad has a perfect balance of tastes and textures. Strips of soft, lightly spiced, fluffy omelette make a delicious contrast with crisp, raw vegetables and sticky Japanese rice.

INGREDIENTS

FOR THE SALAD

⅓ cup (50g) glutinous or sushi rice, cooked

½ cup (50g) snow peas, trimmed and cut into strips

1 yellow pepper, seeded and cut into julienne strips

4 scallions, cut into strips

1 small cucumber, cut into thin strips

1 red pepper, seeded and cut into julienne strips

1 bunch watercress

½ cup (100ml) Vinaigrette (see page 45)

FOR THE OMELETTE

4 eggs

1 tbsp soy sauce

1 inch (2.5cm) piece of fresh ginger, chopped

1 tbsp chopped fresh cilantro

freshly ground pepper

3 tbsp (40g) butter

1 For the salad, combine the rice, vegetables, watercress, and vinaigrette in a salad bowl, toss well, and set aside.

2 For the omelette, beat the eggs with the soy sauce, ginger, cilantro, and pepper.

3 Melt half the butter in an omelette pan over medium heat. When just bubbling, pour in half the egg mixture and swirl to coat the bottom of the pan. Cook for 5 minutes, until golden and just set. Turn and cook the other side in the same way. Transfer to a plate and keep warm. Repeat the process to make a second omelette with the remaining mixture.

4 Arrange the salad on four plates. Slice the omelettes into thin strips, then arrange them on top of each serving of salad.

🕐 **Preparation & cooking time**
50 minutes

◷ **Serves 4**

♡ **Nutritional notes**
calories 370; protein 11g; carbohydrates 6g; total fat 34g, of which saturated fat 10g; fiber 2g; sodium 519mg

CAULIFLOWER SALAD WITH GRILLED PEPPERS

In this recipe sweet, roasted peppers and a punchy dressing made with capers, mustard, tarragon, and horseradish give simple cauliflower a real kick. It is important not to overcook the cauliflower florets because they will soften further as they marinate.

INGREDIENTS

2 peppers (1 red, 1 green), roasted, peeled, and seeded (see page 39)
1 large cauliflower

FOR THE DRESSING

½ cup (100ml) olive oil
2 tbsp tarragon vinegar
1 tbsp capers, drained and rinsed
1 garlic clove, crushed
1 tsp Dijon mustard
1 tbsp grated fresh horseradish
1 tomato, seeded and finely diced
1 tbsp chopped fresh tarragon
salt and freshly ground pepper

1 Cut the peppers into strips and place on a warm plate. Set aside and keep warm.

2 Break the cauliflower into florets and cook them in a pot of boiling, salted water for 2 minutes, until tender, but still firm to the bite.

3 Combine all the ingredients for the dressing in a bowl and add the peppers and cauliflower. Toss the vegetables well to coat them in the dressing and let marinate for 1 hour at room temperature before serving.

Preparation & cooking time
50 minutes, plus 1 hour marinating time

Serves 4

Nutritional notes
calories 299; protein 6g; carbohydrates 9g; total fat 27g, of which saturated fat 4g; fiber 4g; sodium 191mg

PEKING SEAWEED SALAD

Asian food markets are the places to visit to stock up on the ingredients for this salad. Pink ginger is a pickled ginger that is available in jars from Japanese food shops. Wakame seaweed is milder and softer than other seaweeds, but, like all varieties, it is chock-full of nutrients. Hijiki seaweed is a good alternative if wakame is not available.

INGREDIENTS

4¼oz (120g) wakame seaweed, soaked in water for 2 hours, then drained
¼ cucumber, halved, seeded, and sliced
8 red radishes, thinly sliced
¾ cup (75g) mooli radish, thinly sliced
1 small zucchini, thinly sliced
½ cup (50g) pea shoots, optional
¾oz (20g) pink ginger
½lb (200g) mixed salad greens
black or toasted sesame seeds, to serve
salt and freshly ground pepper

FOR THE DRESSING

3 tbsp lime juice
1 tbsp chopped fresh mint
2 tbsp chopped fresh cilantro
pinch of crushed red pepper flakes
2 tbsp light soy sauce
2 tbsp granulated sugar
6 tbsp vegetable oil
1 inch (2.5cm) piece of fresh ginger, grated

1 For the dressing, blend all the ingredients together in a bowl, leave for 20 minutes to allow the flavors to infuse, then strain through a sieve into another bowl. Cover and set aside.

2 Place all the ingredients for the salad, except the mixed greens, in a serving bowl. Mix well, then add the dressing. Cover and let marinate for 1 hour at room temperature.

3 Add the salad greens to the salad and toss well. Sprinkle the sesame seeds on top, season to taste, and serve immediately.

Preparation & cooking time
40 minutes, plus 2 hours soaking time, plus 1 hour marinating time

Serves 4

Nutritional notes
calories 236; protein 7g; carbohydrates 8g; total fat 20g, of which saturated fat 2g; fiber 16g; sodium 1613mg

AVOCADO, PAPAYA & BRIE SALAD

This is a pretty and refreshing salad, topped with toasted cheese croutons. Other white-rinded, soft cheeses, apart from Brie, such as Bonchester or Camembert, would also be appropriate for this recipe.

INGREDIENTS

½ cup (50g) green beans
½lb (200g) mixed salad greens (such as Belgian endive and young spinach)
1 avocado, cut into ½ inch (1cm) slices)
1 papaya, cut into ½ inch (1cm) slices)
4½oz (125g) ripe, but firm, Brie, cut into ¼ inch (5mm) slices
8 slices French bread, toasted
salt and freshly ground pepper

FOR THE DRESSING

4 tbsp olive oil
1 tbsp red wine vinegar
1 tsp Dijon mustard
1 tsp maple syrup
½ tbsp green peppercorns, lightly crushed with a knife

1 Blanch the green beans in boiling, salted water for 4–5 minutes, until tender but still crisp. Drain the beans and refresh them in cold water, then pat them dry.

2 For the dressing, blend all the ingredients together in a bowl and season.

3 Place the salad greens in a bowl with the beans, avocado, and papaya and add the dressing. Toss lightly to coat the leaves, then season. Divide the salad among four plates.

4 Place a slice of Brie on each of the toast slices. Place the toast slices on a baking sheet. Broil for about 1 minutes, until the cheese melts.

5 To serve, place two warm, Brie-topped toasts on top of each salad and serve immediately.

 Preparation & cooking time
25 minutes

Serves 4

Nutritional notes
calories 520; protein 15g; carbohydrates 52g; total fat 29g, of which saturated fat 9g; fiber 4g; sodium 838mg

ULTIMATE VEGETABLE SALAD

A garnish of toasted hazelnuts and a rich, creamy dressing lift this salad into a class of its own. The time to make it is early summer, when the vegetables are young and tender. Serve it as an elegant first course or light lunch.

INGREDIENTS

½lb (250g) green beans
2 carrots, cut into strips
¼ cup (50g) peas, cooked
1 celery stalk, sliced
3 tomatoes, seeded and chopped
¼lb (100g) lettuce leaves
¼ cup (50g) hazelnuts, toasted
10 fresh basil leaves, shredded, to garnish

FOR THE DRESSING

⅔ cup (150ml) crème fraîche
2 tbsp tomato paste
1 tbsp red wine vinegar
½ tsp Dijon mustard
½ garlic clove, crushed
salt and freshly ground pepper

1 Blanch the green beans in boiling, salted water for 4–5 minutes, until tender but still crisp. Drain and refresh in cold water, then pat dry. Blanch the carrots in boiling water for 30 seconds. Drain and refresh in cold water, then pat dry.

2 Mix together the beans, carrots, peas, celery, and tomatoes in a bowl.

3 For the dressing, mix all the ingredients together and season, then leave to infuse for 10 minutes. Pour the dressing over the vegetables, reserving a little for the lettuce leaves. Toss the salad well and season to taste.

4 Toss the lettuce leaves with the reserved dressing. Arrange them on a serving plate and lay the vegetables on top. Sprinkle with toasted hazelnuts and garnish with shredded basil leaves.

Preparation & cooking time
25 minutes

Serves 4

Nutritional notes
calories 214; protein 6g; carbohydrates 12g; total fat 16g, of which saturated fat 5g; fiber 5g; sodium 192mg

*Artichoke, Arugula,
Pepper & Mushroom Salad*

ARTICHOKE, ARUGULA, PEPPER & MUSHROOM SALAD

Try to find only the smallest, most tender artichokes to use in this salad. If they are very small, they will hardly need trimming at all. Slice them as thin as possible for the tastiest results.

INGREDIENTS

4 small globe artichokes

juice of 2 lemons

4 tbsp olive oil

4 fresh lemon balm leaves or basil leaves

1 red pepper, roasted, peeled, seeded (see page 39), and cut into julienne strips

¾ cup (75g) mushrooms, thinly sliced

½ cup (40g) young arugula leaves

salt and cracked black pepper

1 Break the stems off the artichokes. Remove the tough outer leaves and trim the tops to about 1 inch (2.5cm) from the bases, so that just the tender leaves and the hearts are left.

2 Cut the artichokes in half lengthwise, to expose the chokes (hairy inner fibers).

Remove the chokes with a spoon and squeeze lemon juice over the hearts to prevent discoloring.

3 Use a sharp knife to cut each artichoke half into very thin slices: take care as they are delicate.

4 Place the artichoke slices in a bowl with the oil and a little more lemon juice. Add the lemon balm leaves, roasted pepper, and mushrooms and marinate for 15–20 minutes.

5 Place the arugula in a bowl, season lightly with salt, and dress with a little of the artichoke marinade. Gently mix together the artichoke slices, peppers, and mushrooms. Pile onto four serving plates. Scatter the cracked black pepper and the arugula leaves on top.

Preparation time
40 minutes, plus 15–20 minutes marinating time

Serves 4

Nutritional notes
calories 152; protein 7g; carbohydrates 8g; total fat 12g, of which saturated fat 2g; fiber 1g; sodium 156mg

POTATO SALAD WITH SAFFRON LEEKS & MUSTARD

Leeks and saffron are a perfect culinary combination. Here they make the base for an unusual, elegant potato salad. Red or new potatoes are the best to use, but if these are unavailable, any good, waxy variety of potato will do.

INGREDIENTS

¼ tsp saffron strands or ½ tsp powdered saffron

½ cup (100ml) boiling water

salt

¾lb (350g) small leeks, trimmed

1lb (450g) potatoes, scrubbed

½ tsp black mustard seeds

FOR THE DRESSING

1 tsp coarse-grain mustard

2 tbsp white wine vinegar

6 tbsp peanut or vegetable oil

2 tbsp snipped fresh chives

1 Place the saffron in a pot and cover with the boiling water. Add a little salt and bring to a boil. Reduce the heat and simmer for 1 minute, then add the leeks. Simmer the leeks for 2–3 minutes, until tender. Drain and cool.

2 For the dressing, place the mustard and vinegar in a bowl with a little salt. Slowly add the oil, whisking all the time, to form an emulsion, then mix in the snipped chives.

3 Place the potatoes in a pot, cover with cold, salted water, bring to a boil, then reduce the heat. Simmer for 15–20 minutes. Drain, then allow to cool a little before slicing into rounds. Place the potatoes in a bowl and coat with the dressing, reserving a little for the leeks. Let the potatoes cool to room temperature.

4 Toss the leeks well in the reserved dressing and arrange on a serving plate. Pile the potatoes on top, sprinkle with black mustard seeds, and serve at room temperature.

Preparation & cooking time
50 minutes

Serves 4

Nutritional notes
calories 252; protein 4g; carbohydrates 21g; total fat 18g, of which saturated fat 4g; fiber 3g; sodium 146mg

SINGAPORE NOODLE SALAD

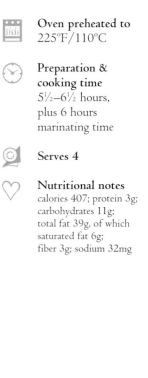

Noodles form the basis of some of the world's best fast-food dishes. Once the vegetables have been sliced, this tasty main course salad can be thrown together in no time at all.

INGREDIENTS

12oz (350g) egg noodles

1/3lb (150g) sugar-snap peas

1 red pepper, halved, seeded, and cut into julienne strips

2 carrots, cut into julienne strips

2 scallions, shredded

1/4lb (100g) shiitake mushrooms, sliced

fresh cilantro leaves

1/2 cup (25g) cashew nuts, toasted

FOR THE DRESSING

4 tbsp peanut oil

1 garlic clove, crushed

1 green chili, halved, seeded, and chopped

3 tbsp rice wine vinegar

1 inch (2.5cm) piece of fresh ginger, grated

1 tbsp hoisin sauce

salt and freshly ground pepper

1 Cook the noodles according to package instructions, drain, and refresh under cold, running water.

2 Blanch the sugar-snap peas in boiling, salted water for 1 minute. Drain and refresh them in cold water, then pat dry. Place all the vegetables except the mushrooms in a bowl. Set aside.

3 For the dressing, heat the oil in a pan, add the garlic and chili, and stir-fry for 30 seconds. Toss in the mushrooms and sauté over high heat for 2 minutes. Remove the mushrooms from the pan and add to the bowl with the vegetables. Add the remaining ingredients for the dressing to the pan and warm through.

4 Pour the dressing over the vegetables and toss. Make a mound of noodles on each serving plate and pile on the vegetables. Alternatively, mix together the dressing, vegetables, and noodles, and pile onto the plates. Top with cilantro and cashew nuts.

Preparation & cooking time
30 minutes

Serves 4

Nutritional notes
calories 536; protein 15g; carbohydrates 75g; total fat 22g, of which saturated fat 5g; fiber 5g; sodium 485mg

CRAZY TOMATO SALAD

Make this in late summer when tomatoes are at their best. Full of concentrated tomato flavor, it combines two different types of fresh tomato with sweet, oven-dried tomatoes that have been infused with oil, basil, garlic, oregano, and coriander seeds.

INGREDIENTS

4–6 plum tomatoes

2/3 cup (150ml) extra virgin olive oil

1/2 tsp coriander seeds

2 garlic cloves, peeled and thinly sliced

8 sprigs fresh basil

1 tbsp fresh oregano leaves

4–6 ripe tomatoes, peeled (see page 39)

16 red cherry tomatoes

2 tbsp red wine vinegar

1/2 tbsp granulated sugar

2/3 cup (150ml) tomato juice

2 tbsp dry vermouth

sea salt and cracked black pepper

1 Cut the plum tomatoes in half lengthwise and lay them out on a baking sheet, with the cut sides facing upward.

2 Season and drizzle with 2 tablespoons of oil. Place in the oven and leave to shrivel gently for 5–6 hours. When cooked, place the oven-dried tomatoes in a pan with the remaining oil, coriander seeds, garlic, basil, and oregano and warm through on very low heat for 15 minutes. Set aside.

3 Cut the ripe and cherry tomatoes in half and add to the pan containing the oven-dried tomatoes. Transfer to a bowl. Combine the vinegar, sugar, tomato juice, and vermouth and pour it over the tomatoes. Cover and marinate at room temperature for 6 hours. Sprinkle with salt and cracked black pepper and serve.

Oven preheated to
225°F/110°C

Preparation & cooking time
5 1/2–6 1/2 hours, plus 6 hours marinating time

Serves 4

Nutritional notes
calories 407; protein 3g; carbohydrates 11g; total fat 39g, of which saturated fat 6g; fiber 3g; sodium 32mg

SALAD FIL FIL

This pleasant-tasting salad originated in North Africa. The name Fil Fil comes from a North African word for green peppers, which are used in this salad. The dish usually does not include couscous, but I like to add it because it gives the salad additional texture. You can serve it with a fresh green salad, if you wish.

INGREDIENTS

½ cup (100g) couscous

4 large green peppers, roasted, peeled, seeded (see page 39), and diced

4 ripe but firm tomatoes, peeled, seeded (see page 39), and diced

2 garlic cloves, crushed

1 fresh green chili, seeded and sliced

2 tbsp chopped fresh parsley

salt and freshly ground pepper

FOR THE DRESSING

6 tbsp olive oil

4 tbsp fresh lemon juice

1 tsp cumin seeds

1 Cook the couscous according to package instructions. When cooked, place in a large bowl and mix in the peppers. Season well.

2 For the dressing, place the olive oil, lemon juice, cumin seeds, and seasoning in a bowl and whisk until well combined.

3 Mix the tomatoes and dressing into the couscous and peppers along with the remaining ingredients. Toss the salad, then check the seasoning.

4 Cover and chill in the refrigerator for up to 2 hours to allow the flavors to develop. Serve lightly chilled.

🕐 **Preparation & cooking time**
50 minutes, plus 2 hours chilling time

◎ **Serves 4**

♡ **Nutritional notes**
calories 253; protein 4g; carbohydrates 21g; total fat 18g, of which saturated fat 3g; fiber 4g; sodium 116mg

MIDDLE EASTERN FLATBREAD & SUMAK SALAD

A salad for the thrifty – this is a great way to use up stale pita bread. Sumak is a spice powder with an astringent, lemony flavor. You should be able to find it in Middle Eastern or specialty food stores.

INGREDIENTS

1 cucumber, chopped

4 tomatoes, chopped

8 scallions, chopped

1 green pepper, halved, seeded, and chopped

½ cup (100g) Great Northern beans, soaked overnight and cooked (see page 41)

12 pitted black olives

½ tbsp sumak

2 pita breads, broken into small pieces

salt and freshly ground pepper

FOR THE DRESSING

1 tbsp finely chopped fresh cilantro

½ tbsp finely chopped mint

1 garlic clove, crushed

8 tbsp olive oil

juice of 2 lemons

1 For the dressing, blend together all the ingredients in a mixing bowl until thoroughly combined.

2 Place all the vegetables in a bowl with the cooked beans, olives, half the sumak, and the dressing. Toss the vegetables to coat them with the dressing. Cover and chill in the refrigerator before serving.

3 In a dry skillet, toast the pita bread pieces, shaking the pan from time to time until they are browned and crisp. Stir into the vegetables and season to taste. Transfer the salad to a serving bowl. Sprinkle the remaining sumak on top and serve.

🕐 **Preparation & cooking time**
1½–2 hours, plus overnight soaking time

◎ **Serves 4**

♡ **Nutritional notes**
calories 414; protein 11g; carbohydrates 40g; total fat 24g, of which saturated fat 4g; fiber 8g; sodium 521mg

PURPLE POTATO, ARTICHOKE & MILLET SALAD

Purple potatoes are the latest designer potatoes. They are a pretty color and make a great addition to my new-look Niçoise salad. It has wonderful red, green, and white colors as well as my favorite grain, millet.

INGREDIENTS

¾ cup (120g) millet
¾lb (300g) purple potatoes
¼lb (120g) Jerusalem artichokes
½ cup (50g) green beans, cooked
¼lb (100g) mixed yellow and red cherry tomatoes
3 hard-boiled eggs, quartered
¼ cup (20g) pitted black olives, halved
2 garlic cloves, crushed
1 tbsp nonpareil capers, drained
2 shallots, finely chopped

FOR THE DRESSING

4 tbsp white wine vinegar
½ cup (125ml) olive oil
3 tbsp (50g) pine nuts, toasted
2 tbsp chopped fresh oregano
2 tbsp chopped fresh chives

1 For the dressing, blend all the ingredients together in a bowl, cover, and set aside.

2 Place the millet in a separate bowl, cover with boiling water, cover the bowl, and let stand for 10–15 minutes. Drain the millet and pat it dry with a cloth.

3 Cook the potatoes whole, in their skins, in a pot of boiling water for 15–20 minutes. Drain. When cool enough, peel and cut into ¼ inch (5mm) slices. Meanwhile, cook the artichokes in boiling water for 15 minutes, peel, and cut into ¼ inch (5mm) slices.

4 Combine all the ingredients in a bowl, add the dressing, mix well, and serve.

Preparation & cooking time
45 minutes

Serves 4

Nutritional notes
calories 627; protein 11g; carbohydrates 43g; total fat 45g, of which saturated fat 6g; fiber 3g; sodium 200mg

GOAT CHEESE & ROASTED SHALLOT SALAD

In this recipe the shallots are roasted with balsamic vinegar for an intensely sweet-sour flavor. They are the perfect partner for the goat cheese, but they are just as good served as an accompaniment to other dishes.

INGREDIENTS

2 goat cheeses, halved crosswise

½lb (250g) small shallots, peeled

½ cup (100ml) balsamic vinegar

1 tbsp granulated sugar

½lb (200g) small beets, cooked and cut into wedges

FOR THE MARINADE

⅔ cup (150ml) olive oil

2 garlic cloves, sliced

1 tbsp chopped fresh thyme

2 tbsp chopped fresh rosemary

½ tsp black peppercorns, crushed

FOR THE DRESSING

½ cup (100ml) orange juice

2 tbsp walnut oil

¼ cup (50g) dried apricots, soaked in water for 2 hours and sliced

1 tbsp walnuts, roughly chopped

1 For the marinade, combine the ingredients in a bowl. Place the goat cheese in a shallow dish and pour the marinade over. Cover and refrigerate overnight.

2 The following day, place the shallots in a roasting pan. Pour the marinade from the cheese over the shallots; set the cheese aside and cover. Add the vinegar to the shallots, and sprinkle with sugar. Bake for 45–50 minutes, until the shallots are tender. Strain the juices left in the pan and reserve. Add the beets to the shallots and return to the oven to keep warm.

3 Blend the dressing ingredients in a small bowl and add the strained juices from the shallots.

4 Place the cheese on a baking sheet under a hot broiler to warm through and soften slightly, but do not let it melt.

5 Place one portion of cheese on each plate and surround with the beets and shallots. Pour the dressing around the cheese and vegetables. Serve at room temperature.

Oven preheated to 400°F/200°C

Preparation & cooking time
1 hour 40 minutes, plus 2 hours soaking time, plus overnight marinating time

Serves 4

Nutritional notes
calories 674; protein 10g; carbohydrates 22g; total fat 61g, of which saturated fat 12g; fiber 3g; sodium 300mg

GREEN SALAD WITH GARDEN HERBS

A good salad must be made with care. Select only the freshest greens, rinse and dry them thoroughly, and toss with the dressing just before serving. The choice of herbs is up to you, but the more delicate varieties, such as chervil and basil, work best in this recipe.

INGREDIENTS

1 small garlic clove, halved

½lb (250g) mixed greens (such as mâche, little gem, arugula, young sorrel leaves, curly endive, and cos)

bunch of mixed fresh herbs (such as basil, tarragon, chervil, flat-leaf parsley, and mint)

4 slices French bread, toasted

1 tbsp Dijon mustard

FOR THE DRESSING

1 shallot, finely chopped

½ tsp herb mustard

2 tbsp Champagne vinegar

salt

½ cup (125ml) extra virgin olive oil

1 Rub the inside of a large bowl liberally with the cut side of the garlic clove. Toss the greens and herbs in the bowl.

2 For the dressing, mix together the shallot, herb mustard, champagne vinegar, and a little salt. Slowly whisk in all but 1 tablespoon of the oil until an emulsion is formed. Drizzle the dressing over the greens and herbs and toss well.

3 Brush the toasted bread slices on both sides with the remaining oil and spread with Dijon mustard. Arrange the toasted bread on top of the salad.

Preparation & cooking time
20 minutes

Serves 4

Nutritional notes
calories 404; protein 5g; carbohydrates 24g; total fat 33g, of which saturated fat 5g; fiber 1g; sodium 261mg

DESSERTS

CHOOSE A DESSERT to complement your main course, or build the rest of your meal around a spectacular finale. Here are recipes for every occasion: refreshing fresh fruit poached in an aromatic spiced syrup; delicate ice creams; luscious tarts; and for chocolate lovers — a rich chocolate tart with chili oil. Desserts are not immune to global influences, and I have included sweet things from the Middle East, Mexico, and the Mediterranean.

SAFFRON PEACHES WITH SUMMER BERRIES

KEY INGREDIENTS

Star anise has an aniseed flavor and interesting shape

Lemon counterbalances the sweetness of desserts with a pleasant tang

Summer berries give a splash of color and sweetness to many desserts

Peaches are sweet and juicy whether eaten raw or lightly poached

Cinnamon gives warmth and sweetness to sweet and savory dishes

Saffron has a rich, yellow color and a pungent, sweet scent

Try to get white peaches for this delicate and refreshing summer dessert; sweeter than yellow ones, their pale flesh makes a pleasing contrast to the scarlet berries.

INGREDIENTS

4 ripe peaches (white, if possible)
½ bottle dry white wine or champagne
1¼ cups (250g) superfine sugar
4 star anise
1 vanilla bean (or 1 tsp vanilla extract)
2 cinnamon sticks
½ lemon, cut into ⅛ inch (3mm) slices
¼ tsp fresh saffron strands
2 cups (220g) mixed summer berries

1 Bring a large pot of water to a boil, add the peaches, and poach for 1–2 minutes. Remove the peaches from the pan and, when cool, peel them carefully.

2 In a separate large pot, combine the wine with 1¼ cups (300ml) water, the sugar, star anise, vanilla bean, cinnamon, lemon, and saffron strands.

3 Boil the liquid until it becomes syrupy, then lower the heat and add the peaches. If there is not enough liquid to cover the peaches, add more water. Cover with a piece of waxed paper and simmer for 15–20 minutes. Remove the peaches and set aside.

4 Raise the heat and boil the syrup until it is reduced by a third. Remove from the heat and let cool for a few minutes before returning the peaches to the pot. Let cool.

5 Place the peaches in a serving bowl and scatter the berries on top. Strain the syrup into a pitcher, reserve the cinnamon and star anise, then pour the syrup over the peaches. Cover and chill for 4 hours. Decorate with the cinnamon and star anise.

Preparation & cooking time
1 hour, plus 4 hours chilling time

Serves 4

Nutritional notes
calories 349; protein 1g; carbohydrates 78g; total fat 0.2g, of which saturated fat 0.03g; fiber 2g; sodium 11mg

HAZELNUT TORTE WITH KIRSCH & BLUEBERRIES

Although this looks complicated to make, it is actually quite simple — a straightforward hazelnut meringue filled with flavored cream and blueberries. Meringue circles can be made up to 24 hours in advance, then kept in an airtight container until ready to use.

INGREDIENTS

FOR THE TORTE

2 egg whites

⅔ cup (125g) superfine sugar

¼ tsp baking powder

1 cup (125g) hazelnuts, coarsely ground

FOR THE KIRSCH CREAM

⅔ cup (150ml) whipping or heavy cream

½ cup (75g) confectioners' sugar

zest and juice of ½ lemon

6 tbsp kirsch

FOR THE BLUEBERRY SAUCE

2 cups (250g) fresh blueberries

½ cup (55g) confectioners' sugar, plus extra, to dust

juice of 1 lemon

blackberry leaves or mint leaves, to decorate

1 For the torte, whisk the egg whites and sugar until standing in stiff peaks. Whisk in the baking powder, then fold in the hazelnuts.

2 Pipe eight circles of the mixture, each measuring about 3 inches (7.5cm), onto baking parchment. Bake for about 30 minutes, until you can lift the circles cleanly off the paper. Cool.

3 For the cream, whisk together the cream and confectioners' sugar until lightly whipped. Add the lemon zest and juice, and the kirsch, and whisk until stiff.

4 For the sauce, in a blender or food processor blend 1¼ cups (150g) of the blueberries with the confectioners' sugar and lemon juice until smooth, then strain through a fine sieve.

5 To serve, pipe the cream onto four meringues, pour over the sauce, and top with the remaining meringues. Decorate with the remaining berries and leaves, and dust with confectioners' sugar.

Oven preheated to 325°F/160°C

Preparation & cooking time 50 minutes

Serves 4

Nutritional notes calories 550; protein 3g; carbohydrates 82g; total fat 22g, of which saturated fat 12g; fiber 2g; sodium 81mg

---

BAKED FIGS WITH DRIED FRUIT & ANISETTE

Dark purple figs have a wonderful flavor and are the best figs for this dish. I like to serve the figs hot, as a contrast to the chilled, vanilla-flavored cream, but they are also very good cold.

INGREDIENTS

½ cup (100g) selection of dried fruit, such as apricots, prunes, dates, and raisins

8 large, ripe, fresh figs

2 tbsp honey or superfine sugar

zest and juice of 1 orange

¼ tsp ground cardamom seeds

pinch of fennel seeds

6 tbsp anisette liqueur, such as Pernod, or brandy (optional)

1 tbsp pine nuts, toasted

fresh mint sprigs, to decorate

TO SERVE

few drops of vanilla extract

½ cup (100ml) crème fraîche or mascarpone

1 In a large bowl, soak the dried fruit in water overnight. Drain, then cut into small pieces.

2 Cut the fresh figs in half, scoop out the centers, then fill each fig half with the dried fruit.

3 Place the figs in a baking dish. Combine the honey, orange zest and juice, cardamom, fennel seeds, and anisette liqueur, if using, and pour over the figs. Cover, then bake for 20 minutes, basting occasionally with the juices.

4 Place the figs on a serving plate, pour the juice over them, and sprinkle the pine nuts on top. Decorate with fresh mint. Stir the vanilla extract into the crème fraîche until well combined and serve with the figs.

Oven preheated to 325°F/160°C

Preparation & cooking time 35 minutes, plus overnight soaking time

Serves 4

Nutritional notes calories 349; protein 4g; carbohydrates 44g; total fat 15g, of which saturated fat 8g; fiber 3g; sodium 35mg

PROSECCO-MASCARPONE & RASPBERRY SYLLABUB

For this luscious dessert, raspberries are marinated in Italian sparkling wine, then topped with a rich, creamy, orange-scented syllabub, and decorated with a sprinkling of white chocolate shavings and crushed amaretti. This is easy to make, and devastatingly good.

INGREDIENTS

1 pint (350g) raspberries

*6 tbsp Prosecco
(or other sparkling white wine)*

9oz (250g) mascarpone

zest and juice of 1 orange

*¼ cup (25g) confectioners' sugar,
or 1 tbsp honey*

4 tbsp sweet white wine

TO DECORATE

2oz (50g) white chocolate shavings

6 amaretti cookies, crushed

1 Place the raspberries in a bowl, pour the Prosecco over them, then cover with plastic wrap and macerate overnight, or for at least 2 hours.

2 Remove a third of the raspberries and push them through a fine sieve to remove any seeds. Add the resulting raspberry puree to the remaining raspberries and mix together gently, then set aside.

3 In a bowl, lightly whisk together the mascarpone, the orange zest and juice, sugar, and sweet white wine. Divide the fruit among four tall, thin glasses. Spoon the mascarpone mixture on top of the fruit.

4 Chill in the refrigerator for about 4 hours. Decorate with the white chocolate shavings and the crushed amaretti cookies before serving.

Preparation time
½ hour, plus
at least 2 hours
macerating time
(preferably overnight),
plus 4 hours
chilling time

Serves 4

Nutritional notes
calories 330; protein 12g;
carbohydrates 45g;
total fat 10g, of which
saturated fat 3g;
fiber 25g; sodium 44mg

PINK GRAPEFRUIT & ROSE WATER GRANITA

This pretty pink granita has an intriguing, exotic taste due to the inclusion of rose water, which was a popular flavoring in Elizabethan England. Rose water is also associated with Middle Eastern cooking, where it is used in both sweet and savory dishes.

INGREDIENTS

2 tbsp (25ml) rose water

½ cup (100g) superfine sugar

freshly grated zest of 1 pink grapefruit

*1¼ cups (300ml) freshly squeezed
pink grapefruit juice*

TO SERVE

pink grapefruit segments (all pith removed)

fresh raspberries

1 Place the rose water and sugar in a pot with 2 cups (425ml) water and bring to a boil. When the liquid has reduced its original volume by almost half, remove from the heat and add the grapefruit zest and juice.

2 Pour into a shallow pan or baking dish and place in the freezer. Every half hour, stir up the mixture roughly with a fork, to give an icy, crystalline texture.

3 Freeze for up to 6 hours before serving. To serve, place two scoops of granita in each bowl and surround with segments of fresh pink grapefruit and fresh raspberries.

Preparation time
30 minutes,
plus 6 hours
freezing time

Serves 8

Nutritional notes
calories 124; protein 1g;
carbohydrates 31g;
total fat 0.3g, of which
saturated fat 0.01g;
fiber 0.7g; sodium 5mg

APPLE & RHUBARB PIZZA

Pizzas have been topped with just about everything from smoked salmon to bacon and eggs, but have you ever tried a sweet pizza? In this recipe, the pizza is topped with a ginger-spiced rhubarb puree and thin slices of caramelized apple. Serve with Rhubarb Sorbet (see below).

INGREDIENTS

FOR THE PIZZA BASE

1 cake (15g) fresh yeast
or 1 envelope dry yeast

⅔ cup (150ml) lukewarm water

2 cups (225g) all-purpose flour

4 tbsp superfine sugar, plus extra to sprinkle

FOR THE RHUBARB TOPPING

¾lb (300g) rhubarb, cubed

2 tbsp (50g) superfine sugar

½oz (15g) stem ginger, finely chopped

FOR THE APPLE TOPPING

4 apples, peeled, cored, and thinly sliced

3 tbsp (50g) unsalted butter, melted

Rhubarb Sorbet (see below), to serve

1 For the pizza base, dissolve the yeast in the water and, when frothy, pour onto the flour and sugar in a bowl. Stir to combine, then knead to form a smooth dough. Cover the bowl with a damp cloth and leave for 20–30 minutes in a warm place until doubled in size.

2 Meanwhile, place the rhubarb in a medium pot with the sugar and ginger. Bring to a boil, lower the heat, and simmer for 20–25 minutes, until nearly all the liquid has evaporated and the rhubarb is syrupy. Let cool.

3 When the dough has risen, punch it down by pushing it with your fists. Roll out the dough into one large rectangle. Place on a sheet of baking parchment on a baking sheet.

4 Spread the rhubarb evenly over the base, then lay the apple slices, overlapping, over the top. Brush the pizza with melted butter and leave in a warm place to rise for 30 minutes longer. Sprinkle with a little superfine sugar and bake for 20–25 minutes, until the apples are golden and the pizza is crisp. Serve with rhubarb sorbet (see below), if desired.

 Oven preheated to 400°F/200°C

Preparation & cooking time 1–1¼ hours, plus 1 hour rising time

Serves 6

Nutritional notes calories 319; protein 5g; carbohydrates 61g; total fat 8g, of which saturated fat 5g; fiber 3g; sodium 7mg

RHUBARB SORBET

Rhubarb has a slight image problem, perhaps because many of us were forced to eat stewed rhubarb when we were children. Young, pink rhubarb has a much better flavor than the coarse old stems, and makes a very refreshing sorbet. This sorbet is particularly good served with the Apple & Rhubarb Pizza (see above).

INGREDIENTS

1 cup (250g) superfine sugar

½lb (250g) rhubarb, chopped

juice of 1 lemon

1 Place all the ingredients in a heavy-bottomed pan with 2¼ cups (500ml) water and bring to a boil. Lower the heat, then simmer for about 10 minutes, until the rhubarb is well cooked and the liquid is syrupy.

2 Transfer the mixture to a blender or food processor and blend until smooth. Put the mixture in a bowl and leave until thoroughly cooled.

3 Pour the mixture into an ice cream maker and freeze according to the manufacturer's instructions. If you do not have an ice cream maker, place the mixture in a plastic freezer box. Cover the box and freeze for 3–4 hours, until half frozen. Beat the mixture with a handheld electric beater; freeze for 3 hours longer. Whisk again, then freeze for 4–6 hours before serving.

Preparation time 35 minutes, plus 10–13 hours freezing time

Serves 8

Nutritional notes calories 125; protein 0.3g; carbohydrates 33g; total fat 0.03g, of which saturated fat 0g; fiber 0.4g; sodium 3mg

CHOCOLATE & CHILI OIL TART

This is not as strange as it sounds. Mexican cooks often include a little chocolate in spicy dishes, so I decided to turn the tables and add chili oil to chocolate. It gives a warmth and depth of flavor that counterbalances the sweetness beautifully. This is one of my favorite desserts.

INGREDIENTS

FOR THE WALNUT PASTRY

2¼ cups (250g) all-purpose flour

½ cup (50g) ground walnuts

¼ cup (75g) superfine sugar

11 tbsp (150g) softened unsalted butter, plus extra, to grease

1 egg, beaten

FOR THE FILLING

2 eggs, beaten

6 egg yolks, beaten

¼ cup (70g) superfine sugar

13oz (370g) dark chocolate

1 tsp chili oil

½lb (250g) unsalted butter

confectioners' sugar, to dust

1 For the pastry, sift the flour into a bowl, add the walnuts, sugar, and butter and stir until the mixture forms crumbs. Add the egg, stir to bind the ingredients together, and gently knead to a smooth pastry. Cover and chill in the refrigerator for at least 4 hours.

2 Grease an 8–9 inch (20–23cm) tart pan. Roll out the pastry to line the tart pan; allow a ½ inch (1cm) overlap. Cover with waxed paper, fill with baking beans, and place on a baking sheet.

3 Bake blind for 10 minutes. Remove the baking beans and paper and bake for 10 minutes more. If there are any cracks in the pastry, seal with beaten egg and bake for 2 minutes more. Cool.

4 For the filling, beat together the eggs, egg yolks, and sugar in a bowl. Melt the chocolate in a bowl over a pan of simmering water (making sure that the water does not touch the bowl). When it has melted, add the oil and butter and mix well. Stir into the eggs.

5 Pour the chocolate mixture into the tart shell and bake for 10 minutes, until set. Remove from the pan. Dust with confectioners' sugar and serve when cooled.

Oven preheated to 400°F/200°C

Preparation & cooking time
1–1¼ hours, plus 4 hours chilling time

Serves 8

Nutritional notes
calories 915; protein 12g; carbohydrates 74g; total fat 66g, of which saturated fat 37g; fiber 2g; sodium 49mg

BUTTERNUT SOUFFLE WITH BLACKBERRIES

This is a new twist on an old favorite. Here I use shallow pans as the cooking vessels, rather than the more usual soufflé dish. I think that this adds a little more elegance to the soufflé and, nestled on a tart blackberry sauce, it is a flavor sensation.

Oven preheated to
375°F/190°C

Preparation &
cooking time
1 hour 20 minutes

Serves 8

Nutritional notes
calories 251; protein 8g;
carbohydrates 32g;
total fat 10g, of which
saturated fat 5g;
fiber 2g; sodium 86mg

INGREDIENTS

6oz (175g) peeled butternut squash, chopped

3 tbsp (40g) unsalted butter,
plus extra, to grease

⅓ cup (40g) unbleached flour

zest of 1 orange

3 tbsp Grand Marnier
(or other orange liqueur)

1¾ cups (400ml) hot milk

5 eggs, separated

⅓ cup (85g) superfine sugar

⅓ cup (15g) cornstarch

FOR THE BLACKBERRY SAUCE

2½ cups (300g) blackberries

½ cup (50g) confectioners' sugar

juice of ½ lemon

julienne of orange zest, to decorate

1 Place the squash in a pan with 1 cup (250ml) water, bring to a boil, then simmer for 15 minutes, until soft. Drain, then blend or finely mash the squash until smooth. Let cool.

2 Melt the butter in a pan over medium heat, then beat in the flour, using a wooden spoon, until the mixture leaves the sides of the pan. Add the squash puree, orange zest, and Grand Marnier and beat thoroughly until well combined.

3 Gradually pour the hot milk into the pan, beating all the time, and cook over low heat for 5 minutes, stirring often. Pour into a large bowl, then let cool slightly before beating in the egg yolks, one at a time. Set aside.

4 Whisk together the egg whites, sugar, and cornstarch until standing in stiff peaks. Beat one third of the whites into the squash mixture, then gently fold in the remaining two thirds with a spatula until well combined.

5 Grease eight crepe pans or eight individual nonstick tart pans, 3 inches (7cm) in diameter. Dust the bottoms and sides with superfine sugar, then fill two thirds full with the soufflé mix. Place the crepe pans in the oven or, if using the tartlet pans, place in a shallow baking pan and pour in hot water to come a third of the way up the sides of the pans. Bake for 15–20 minutes, until the soufflés have risen and are golden.

6 For the sauce, blend together 1¾ cups (200g) blackberries, the confectioners' sugar, and lemon juice in a blender or food processor, then strain through a fine sieve.

7 Pour a little sauce onto each plate, top with the remaining whole blackberries, then place the soufflés on top, straight from the oven. Scatter the julienne of orange zest around the outside, dust with sugar, and serve.

ALMOND & HONEY FUDGE TART

The rich almond-studded fudge filling makes this a dessert to savor. This truly is a pièce de résistance.

INGREDIENTS

FOR THE PASTRY

3 cups (350g) all-purpose flour

pinch of salt

2 tbsp confectioners' sugar

½ lb (250g) cold, unsalted butter, cut into pieces, plus extra, to grease

FOR THE FILLING

1¼ cups (275g) superfine sugar

2 cups (225g) blanched whole almonds

7 tbsp (100g) unsalted butter

⅔ cup (150ml) milk

2 tbsp honey

1 For the pastry, sift the flour, salt, and sugar into a large bowl. Cut the butter into the flour with a knife, then rub it into the mixture until it resembles fine bread crumbs. Sprinkle in enough cold water to bind the mixture. Gather the pastry into a ball. Cover and refrigerate for 1 hour.

2 Meanwhile, for the filling, bring the sugar and ⅔ cup (150ml) water to a boil and stir until the sugar has dissolved. Boil rapidly for about 5 minutes, until the mixture begins to caramelize.

3 When pale brown, remove from the heat. Stir in the almonds and butter, then stir in the milk. Return to a low heat and simmer for 15–20 minutes, until the mixture becomes quite thick. Remove from the heat and stir in the honey. Let cool slightly.

4 Meanwhile, lightly grease an 8–9 inch (20–23cm) tart pan. Roll out two thirds of the dough and use to line the pan. Prick the bottom. Pour in the filling. Cover with the remaining dough, dampen the edges with water, and press to seal them. Make a small vent in the center. Bake for 40 minutes, until golden. Cool before serving.

Oven preheated to 400°F/200°C

Preparation & cooking time 1½ hours, plus 1 hour chilling time

Serves 10

Nutritional notes calories 668; protein 9g; carbohydrates 67g; total fat 43g, of which saturated fat 20g; fiber 3g; sodium 97mg

CHILLED MELON & SAGO SOUP

This is an Asian-inspired soup, served in individual melons. It is important to achieve the right balance of sweet and sour, so keep tasting as you add the lime juice and maple syrup. If you wish, you can scoop out the melon flesh and blend it together with the milk in a blender or food processor, but I prefer to eat the soup first and the melon later.

INGREDIENTS

4 small galia melons

wedge of watermelon, cut into ½ inch (1cm) cubes

wedge of honeydew melon, cut into ½ inch (1cm) cubes

FOR THE SOUP

1½ cups (200g) pearl sago

1¼ cups (300ml) milk

⅔ cup (150ml) coconut milk

¼ cup (50ml) heavy cream

juice of 1 lime

maple syrup, to taste

1 Cut a thin slice off the base of each whole melon so that it sits upright. Slice the top off each one about 1½ inches (4cm) down. Remove the seeds from inside each melon with a large metal spoon. Refrigerate the melon shells while you prepare the soup.

2 For the soup, place the sago in a pan, cover with water, and bring to a boil. Reduce the heat and simmer for 40–45 minutes, stirring regularly. When cooked, refresh under cold running water. Drain well and leave until cold.

3 In a bowl, mix together the milk, coconut milk, and cream, then add the lime juice and maple syrup to sweeten to your taste. Finally, add the sago and mix together. Chill the soup for up to 4 hours in the refrigerator. Divide the cubes of melon among the melon shells, then divide the soup among the shells. Serve chilled.

Preparation time 1 hour, plus 4 hours chilling time

Serves 4

Nutritional notes calories 363; protein 3g; carbohydrates 73g; total fat 8g, of which saturated fat 5g; fiber 0.9g; sodium 124mg

SWEET OAT TART

For me, the secret of this "comfort food" tart is to include lots of lemon juice to offset the sweetness. The filling is a delicious, wholesome mixture, similar to pancakes.

INGREDIENTS

butter, to grease
½ batch Sweet Pastry (see page 42)
1¼ cups (300ml) golden syrup
½ cup (75g) rolled oats
zest and juice of 1 large lemon
pinch of ground ginger

1 Grease an 8 inch (20cm) tart pan. Roll out the pastry and use it to line the pan.

2 Warm the golden syrup gently in a medium pan over low heat. Stir in the rolled oats, then the lemon zest and juice, and the ginger. Heat gently until the mixture is slightly runny in texture.

3 Pour the mixture into the prepared pastry shell and bake for about 25 minutes. Let cool for 10–15 minutes: the filling will firm up as it cools. Serve the tart warm.

Oven preheated to 400°F/200°C

Preparation & cooking time 1 hour, plus 40 minutes for the pastry

Serves 4

Nutritional notes calories 546; protein 6g; carbohydrates 100g; total fat 17g, of which saturated fat 9g; fiber 2g; sodium 219mg

FROZEN LEMON YOGURT & PEPPER CHERRIES

This tangy yogurt dessert goes back a long way in my repertoire, although the pepper cherries are a new addition. The peppercorns add an extra bite to the sweet cherry compote.

INGREDIENTS

2 eggs
¼ cup (50g) superfine sugar
zest and juice of 3 lemons
½ cup (125g) plain yogurt
⅓ cup (75ml) heavy cream, lightly whipped
FOR THE CHERRY COMPOTE
⅓ cup (75g) superfine sugar
2 tbsp (25g) unsalted butter
½ tbsp lemon juice
1 tsp green peppercorns
1 lb (450g) pitted fresh cherries
maraschino liqueur or kirsch, to taste (optional)
mint leaves, to decorate

1 Place the eggs, sugar, and lemon zest and juice in a bowl and set over a pan of simmering water, making sure that the water is not touching the bottom of the bowl. Whisk until the mixture is pale and thick and has doubled in volume.

2 Remove the bowl from the pan and continue to whisk until the mixture cools. When cool, fold in the yogurt gently with a metal spoon, then lightly fold in the whipped cream.

3 Place four 2 inch (5cm) metal ring molds, or individual ramekins, on a baking sheet. Fill with the yogurt cream and smooth the tops with a knife. Freeze for 3 hours before serving.

4 For the cherry compote, heat the sugar, butter, lemon juice, and peppercorns over high heat until the sugar and butter lightly caramelize. Add the cherries and liqueur, if using, then put a flame to the sauce to burn off the alcohol. Reduce the heat, add 4 tablespoons of water, and simmer the cherries until just soft.

5 Loosen the yogurt from the molds with a thin-bladed knife. Turn out onto serving plates. Pour the cherry compote over the yogurt and decorate with mint leaves.

Preparation time 30 minutes, plus 3 hours freezing time

Serves 4

Nutritional notes calories 403; protein 7g; carbohydrates 50g; total fat 20g, of which saturated fat 11g; fiber 1g; sodium 100mg

Note: this recipe contains uncooked egg.

WINTER TRIFLE

This unusual trifle is made with caramelized pears and a light sponge layer that has been flavored with coffee and rum, just like an Italian tiramisù. You may be worried about using custard powder, but I use it a lot in desserts. It is a good, convenient product and should not be ignored.

INGREDIENTS

½ cup (100g) superfine sugar

4 large pears, peeled, cored, and cut horizontally in ¼ inch (5mm) thick slices

2 tbsp dark rum

2 tbsp coffee extract

24 ladyfingers or 1 sponge cake, cut into ¾ inch (2cm) cubes

½ cup (100ml) heavy cream, lightly whipped

FOR THE CUSTARD

2½ cups (600ml) milk

3 tbsp custard powder

1 tbsp superfine sugar

TO DECORATE

toasted hazelnuts

mint leaves

1 In a heavy-bottomed pan, heat the sugar over high heat until it caramelizes. Add the pears and turn them until they are soft and golden and are coated in the caramel. Remove the pears and put in a bowl. Stir ½ cup (100ml) water, the rum, and the coffee into the syrup, then pour the mixture over the ladyfingers in a bowl.

2 For the custard, mix a little milk with the custard powder. Stir to a paste. Bring the remaining milk and sugar nearly to a boil, then pour onto the paste, stirring. Return the custard to the pan and bring to a boil, stirring. Lower the heat and cook for 1–2 minutes, still stirring. Pour into a bowl, cool, then cover with plastic wrap.

3 Place a few ladyfingers in the bottom of each of four glasses, top with pear slices, then some custard; repeat these layers. Finish with a layer of whipped cream. Serve chilled, decorated with toasted hazelnuts and mint leaves.

Preparation & cooking time
40 minutes, plus 2 hours chilling time

Serves 4

Nutritional notes
calories 648; protein 10g; carbohydrates 103g; total fat 22g, of which saturated fat 11g; fiber 4g; sodium 210mg

ITALIAN CREME CARAMEL

This is a version of crème caramel that I borrowed from a friend of mine. The recipe has been in his family for years. The chocolate is delicate and subtle — an interesting variation on the original.

INGREDIENTS

FOR THE BASE CARAMEL

½ cup (100g) superfine sugar

vegetable oil, for greasing

FOR THE CREME

2¼ cups (500ml) milk

½ vanilla bean, split down the middle

1¼oz (35g) white chocolate

3 eggs

1 egg yolk

⅓ cup (85g) superfine sugar

TO SERVE

1 orange, segmented

2 pints fresh raspberries

white chocolate leaves, or shavings

1 For the caramel, heat the sugar in a heavy-bottomed pan. When it starts to melt, begin to stir slowly but constantly. When dissolved, add 3 tablespoons of water and stir until syrupy. Pour ⅛ inch (3mm) of caramel into each of six lightly greased dariole molds.

2 For the crème, heat the milk with the vanilla bean and bring to a boil. Remove from the heat, add the chocolate, and allow to melt off the heat.

3 In a bowl, whisk together the eggs, egg yolk, and sugar, then slowly pour into the milk mixture, stirring. To prevent the eggs from curdling, make sure that the milk is not too hot. Remove the vanilla bean. Strain the mixture through a fine sieve.

4 Divide the crème among the molds, then place in a deep baking dish. Pour in boiling water to come two thirds of the way up the sides. Bake for 20–25 minutes.

5 Cool, then chill in the refrigerator for 2 hours. Turn out the crème caramel onto serving plates. Pour any caramel left in the molds over the top. Serve with orange segments, raspberries, and chocolate leaves.

Oven preheated to 300°F/150°C

Preparation & cooking time 50 minutes, plus 2 hours chilling time

Serves 6

Nutritional notes calories 454; protein 9g; carbohydrates 84g; total fat 11g, of which saturated fat 5g; fiber 3g; sodium 108mg

CANDIED EGGPLANT & CARDAMOM ICE CREAM

Eggplant may seem an unlikely ingredient for a dessert, but it is often candied or made into sweet preserves in the Middle East. Here, it is combined with another Eastern flavor, cardamom, to make a fragrant but fresh-tasting dessert. If you do not have an ice cream maker, follow the recipe for Rhubarb Sorbet (see page 128).

INGREDIENTS

¼lb (150g) eggplant, cut into small cubes

1¼ cups (250g) superfine sugar

2 tbsp aniseed liqueur (optional)

2¼ cups (500ml) milk

1 cup (250ml) heavy cream

10 fresh cardamom pods, split

1 egg

4 egg yolks

1 Place the eggplant and 3 tbsp (50g) sugar in a pan and cook over high heat for 5–8 minutes, until the eggplant turns golden. Add 1 cup (200ml) water and the liqueur, if using, and simmer for 10 minutes until

the eggplant is soft and the water absorbed. Set aside.

2 Bring the milk, cream, and cardamom to a boil; set aside. Whisk the egg, egg yolks, and remaining sugar in a bowl until fluffy. Pour in the hot milk a little at a time, whisking constantly.

3 Return to the pan and stir over low heat until the mixture thickens enough to coat the back of the spoon. Let cool completely, then chill thoroughly. Strain onto the eggplant, and whisk until smooth. Pour into an ice cream maker and freeze according to the manufacturer's instructions.

Preparation time 50 minutes, plus 10–13 hours freezing time

Serves 6

Nutritional notes calories 610; protein 7g; carbohydrates 86g; total fat 28g, of which saturated fat 16g; fiber 0.5g; sodium 86mg

BREAKFASTS & BRUNCHES

WHAT BETTER WAY to start the day than with a satisfying meal that can be prepared quickly, then savored slowly? Here are a few ideas for some appetizing, energy-giving breakfasts and brunches. Mexican scrambled eggs, vegetarian kedgeree, Blueberry Pancakes, French toast, and fruit-filled popovers are just a few of the international flavors in this section. I like to combine sweet dishes with savory and spicy ones to create an interesting, full-blown brunch spread.

SIMPLE HUEVOS RANCHEROS

KEY INGREDIENTS

Black beans are shiny, black, kidney-shaped beans, often used in Mexican cooking

Avocado is a soft, pear-shaped fruit, rich in oils and vitamins

Fresh cilantro is a very popular herb with a strong flavor

Sour cream has a piquant taste and is excellent in dressings and creamy dips

Tomatoes have a wonderful, sweet flavor and are indispensable as a salsa ingredient

Limes are sour, almost perfumed, citrus fruit, and their juice gives a distinct taste to sauces and salsas

Corn tortillas are made from cornmeal and are usually served deep-fried with a variety of fillings

One of the classics of Mexican cooking, this can be as soothing or as spicy as you like, depending on how many chilies you add to the sauce. My preference is for a fairly substantial number. Cook the beans the night before to save time the following morning.

INGREDIENTS

vegetable oil, for deep-frying
4 corn tortillas
½ cup (75g) black beans, soaked overnight and cooked (see page 41), then mashed
4 eggs
1 avocado, peeled and diced
4 tbsp sour cream
salt and freshly ground pepper
FOR THE SALSA
1 medium tomato, chopped
½ small onion, chopped
½ garlic clove, crushed
1 small red chili, finely chopped
1 tbsp chopped fresh cilantro, plus leaves, to garnish
2 tbsp lime juice
1 tbsp maple syrup
4 tbsp olive oil
drop of Tabasco

1 For the salsa, mix together all the ingredients in a bowl and marinate for up to 30 minutes before using.

2 Heat the vegetable oil in a pan. When hot, deep-fry the corn tortillas for 30 seconds, until golden and crispy. Transfer to a plate and keep warm. Heat a little more oil in a separate skillet and cook the black beans for 1 minute, over high heat, stirring. Set aside and keep warm. Finally, fry the eggs.

3 Place a tortilla on each plate, spoon a generous portion of black beans on top, then add a fried egg. Scatter some diced avocado over each egg. Spoon a little sour cream on top, drizzle the salsa around, then season. Garnish with cilantro.

Preparation & cooking time
1½–2 hours, plus overnight soaking time, plus 30 minutes marinating time

Serves 4

Nutritional notes
calories 591; protein 19g; carbohydrates 48g; total fat 37g, of which saturated fat 9g; fiber 3g; sodium 379mg

SWEET POPOVERS WITH SPICED FRUIT COMPOTE

The fruit compote and batter for this recipe can be prepared the night before, then kept in the refrigerator. All you have to do in the morning is cook the popovers and enjoy a healthy, relaxing breakfast.

INGREDIENTS

1½ cups (175g) all-purpose flour, sifted	
pinch of salt	
1 tbsp superfine sugar	
2 eggs	
1½ cups (300ml) milk	
3 tbsp (40g) unsalted butter, melted	
4 tsp vegetable oil	

FOR THE COMPOTE

2 tbsp maple syrup	
1 cinnamon stick	
2 cloves	
zest and juice of 2 oranges	
¼lb (100g) dried apricots	
¼lb (100g) dried figs	
¼lb (100g) dried prunes	
2 tbsp golden raisins	
2 tbsp (25g) pine nuts, toasted	
confectioners' sugar, to dust	
crème fraîche, to serve	

1 Beat together the flour, salt, sugar, eggs, milk, and butter, until the mixture forms a batter. Let rest for 20 minutes.

2 Meanwhile, for the compote, place the maple syrup, cinnamon, and cloves in a pot with 2 cups (450ml) water. Add the orange zest and juice, and the apricots, figs, and prunes. Bring to a boil, then reduce the heat and simmer for 10 minutes before stirring in the raisins.

3 Lift out the fruit and spices and set aside. Heat the juices over medium heat until light and syrupy. Remove from the heat, return the fruit to the syrup, discard the spices, and add the pine nuts. Cool in the pot.

4 Pour 1 teaspoon of oil into each section of a four-muffin pan and heat in the oven for 3 minutes. Divide the batter among the four muffin cups. Bake for 15 minutes. Reduce the heat to 350°F/180°C and cook for 10 minutes more, until the popovers are golden and puffy. Fill each one with the compote, then dust with sugar. Serve with a generous spoonful of crème fraîche.

Oven preheated to 400°F/200°C

Preparation & cooking time 1 hour

Serves 4

Nutritional notes calories 697; protein 15g; carbohydrates 89g; total fat 34g, of which saturated fat 12g; fiber 6g; sodium 291mg

BLUEBERRY PANCAKES WITH MAPLE SYRUP

This is the ultimate deluxe version of that great breakfast staple — buttermilk pancakes. Stack them high on top of each other, diner style, and pour on a generous portion of maple syrup. Make sure that you buy the genuine article, not maple-flavored syrup, which is a synthetic concoction.

INGREDIENTS

1 cup (125g) all-purpose flour
2 tsp superfine sugar
1 tsp baking powder
½ tsp salt
1 cup (250ml) milk or buttermilk
3 tbsp (40g) unsalted butter, melted
1 egg, lightly beaten
½ cup (50g) pecans, roughly chopped
½ cup (75g) fresh blueberries, plus extra, to garnish
vegetable oil

FOR THE SYRUP

⅔ cup (150ml) maple syrup
1 tbsp ground cinnamon

1 Combine the dry ingredients in a mixing bowl. Make a well in the center, and add the milk, butter, and egg. Gradually fold in the dry ingredients, then whisk until the mixture forms a smooth batter. Cover and let rest for 1 hour. Mix in the pecans and blueberries.

2 Lightly brush a skillet with oil. Heat the oil over high heat, then pour a small ladleful of batter into the pan. Swirl to coat the pan with the batter and cook for 1–2 minutes on each side. Remove and keep warm. Repeat with the remaining batter to make 12 pancakes.

3 Heat the maple syrup and cinnamon in a pan. Bring to a boil, reduce the heat, then simmer for 2 minutes. Let cool. Arrange three pancakes on each plate. Garnish each plate with blueberries and serve with the cinnamon-infused maple syrup poured over the top.

Preparation & cooking time
25 minutes, plus
1 hour resting time

Serves 4

Nutritional notes
calories 559; protein 9g;
carbohydrates 60g;
total fat 33g, of which
saturated fat 10g;
fiber 2g; sodium 285mg

STUFFED FRENCH TOAST

French toast is a great comfort food, but sandwiched together with summer berries and crème fraîche, it makes an elegant brunch dish. You could also serve this as a dessert.

INGREDIENTS

2 eggs
⅔ cup (150ml) light cream or milk
1 tbsp superfine sugar
zest of ½ orange
¼ tsp ground cinnamon
4 slices French bread
3 tbsp (50g) unsalted butter
crème fraîche or ricotta, to serve

FOR THE FILLING

½ cup (100g) fresh raspberries, pureed
confectioners' sugar, to taste
½ pint (150g) selection summer berries (raspberries, strawberries, and blackberries)

1 For the filling, put the raspberry puree in a pan and stir in a little sugar, to taste. Add the other berries and cook over low heat for 15 minutes until the fruit just begins to soften.

2 Beat together the eggs, cream, sugar, orange zest, and cinnamon in a shallow dish. Dip each slice of bread in the egg mixture until soaked through.

3 Heat the butter in a skillet over medium heat until sizzling. Cook the bread slices for 2–3 minutes on each side, until lightly browned. Remove each slice from the skillet and cut in half diagonally.

4 Place half a slice of toast on each serving plate. Divide the warmed summer fruit among them and add a spoonful of crème fraîche to each. Top with the remaining half slices of toast and dust generously with confectioners' sugar, and serve.

Preparation & cooking time
30 minutes

Serves 4

Nutritional notes
calories 351; protein 11g;
carbohydrates 30g;
total fat 22g, of which
saturated fat 13g;
fiber 2g; sodium 373mg

SOY WAFFLES WITH PLUM COMPOTE

You will need a waffle iron for this recipe. If you do not have one, however, you could make pancakes with the batter instead. Sandwich the pancakes together with the compote and cream cheese, in the same way as the waffles.

INGREDIENTS

2 cups (225g) all-purpose flour
1 tbsp baking powder
½ tsp salt
1 tbsp superfine sugar
2 eggs, separated
1½ cups (350ml) soy milk
4 tbsp (75g) unsalted butter, melted
5oz (150ml) cream cheese
confectioners' sugar, to dust

FOR THE PLUM COMPOTE

½lb (250g) ripe plums, halved, pits removed
3 tbsp (50g) superfine sugar
1 cinnamon stick
drop of vanilla extract

1 For the plum compote, place the plums, sugar, cinnamon, and vanilla extract in a pot and covet with water so that the fruit is just submerged. Bring to a boil, reduce the heat, and simmer gently, stirring occasionally, for about 30 minutes, until the plums are plump and tender. Taste the resulting liquid and adjust the sugar to taste. Allow to cool and discard the cinnamon stick.

2 For the waffles, sift the flour, baking powder, salt, and sugar into a bowl. In a separate bowl, lightly beat the egg yolks and milk, then stir in the butter. Make a well in the center of the dry ingredients and pour in the egg mixture. Whisk together to form a smooth batter.

3 Beat the egg whites until stiff and gently fold into the batter with a spatula. Use the batter to cook eight waffles on your waffle iron.

4 To serve, place one waffle on each serving plate, top with the plum compote and a dollop of cream cheese, place another waffle on top, then dust liberally with confectioners' sugar.

Preparation & cooking time
1¼ hours

Serves 4

Nutritional notes
calories 665; protein 14g; carbohydrates 70g; total fat 39g, of which saturated fat 23g; fiber 3g; sodium 927mg

LANESBOROUGH GRANOLA

This is made regularly for our guests at The Lanesborough Hotel in London and is always popular. Vary it by adding different nuts, sunflower or pumpkin seeds, or a touch of ground mixed spice or nutmeg. You could also stir in raisins or other dried fruit once you have broken up the granola.

INGREDIENTS

3 tbsp (50g) unsalted butter
¼ cup (50g) brown sugar
4 tbsp honey
2 tbsp golden syrup
4 drops of vanilla extract
½ cup (75g) slivered almonds
½ cup (75g) pecans, coarsely chopped
2 tbsp (25g) pistachio nuts (optional)
3 cups (375g) rolled oats
2 tbsp (25g) dried coconut

1 Heat the butter in a large pan, add the sugar, honey, golden syrup, and vanilla extract and bring to a boil.

2 Reduce the heat. Stir in the nuts, oats, and coconut. Pour the mixture onto a large baking sheet and spread it out evenly. Bake for 20–25 minutes, until golden, turning the mixture regularly with a wooden spoon.

3 Turn the mixture out onto a clean work surface and leave for about 1 hour to get cold and hard, turning occasionally.

4 Cover the granola with a clean dish towel and bash it with a kitchen mallet or rolling pin to break it up into fairly small pieces. Store in an airtight container at room temperature for up to 4 weeks.

Oven preheated to
375°F/190°C

Preparation & cooking time
40 minutes, plus 1 hour cooling time

Makes 1½ cups (300g)

Nutritional notes
calories 359; protein 8g; carbohydrates 41g; total fat 20g, of which saturated fat 5g; fiber 4g; sodium 75mg

MY FAVORITE MUESLI

This is a simple, light start to the morning, worth getting out of bed for, in fact. For a nice variation, replace the rolled oats with wheat germ and use a flavored yogurt instead of a plain one.

INGREDIENTS

1 cup (125g) rolled oats
⅔ cup (150ml) whipping cream
⅔ cup (150ml) plain yogurt
2 tbsp honey
3 Granny Smith apples, skin left on, cored and coarsely grated
2 tbsp slivered almonds
2 tbsp lemon juice
selection of fresh fruit (bananas, grapes, strawberries, raspberries), to serve

1 Place the oats in a bowl and cover with boiling water. Cover the bowl loosely with a clean dish towel and soak overnight at room temperature.

2 The following day, drain the oats thoroughly, mix in the remaining ingredients, place in a bowl, and serve with some fresh fruit of your choice.

🕐 **Preparation & cooking time**
15 minutes, plus overnight soaking time

⏱ **Serves 4**

♡ **Nutritional notes**
calories 446; protein 9g; carbohydrates 54g; total fat 23g, of which saturated fat 10g; fiber 5g; sodium 62mg

EGG KEDGEREE

This is a kedgeree with a difference since it is served at room temperature rather than hot, and brown rice is used instead of white. The rice adds a good, nutty flavor to the dish. The dressing can be made spicier if you wish, according to individual taste.

INGREDIENTS

1¼ cups (250g) long-grain brown rice
1 small cauliflower, cut into small florets
6 scallions, shredded
¾ cup (200g) canned chickpeas, drained and rinsed
½ cup (50g) cashew nuts, toasted
4 hard-boiled eggs, shelled and halved
fresh cilantro leaves, to garnish
lemon wedges, to serve

FOR THE DRESSING

1 tsp curry paste
5 tbsp vegetable oil
2 tbsp chopped fresh cilantro
1 inch (2.5cm) piece of fresh ginger, grated
juice of 1 lemon

1 Cook the brown rice in a large pot of boiling water for 20–25 minutes, until tender. Drain it well, then rinse under cold, running water and drain again.

2 Cook the cauliflower for 5 minutes in boiling, salted water until just tender. Drain and refresh in cold water. Place the rice and cauliflower in a bowl. Add the scallions, chickpeas, and cashew nuts and mix well.

3 For the dressing, blend all the ingredients together, then toss with the rice. Transfer to a salad bowl and arrange the eggs on top. Garnish with fresh cilantro, add the lemon wedges, and serve at room temperature.

🕐 **Preparation & cooking time**
45 minutes

 Serves 4

♡ **Nutritional notes**
calories 626; protein 19g; carbohydrates 64g; total fat 34g, of which saturated fat 5g; fiber 5g; sodium 197mg

LEEK & BEAN HASH WITH CILANTRO MOJO

Take your time in preparing this dish on a lazy Sunday morning and serve it when your appetite has picked up. You will find that this substantial vegetable hash, with its chili and cilantro topping, makes a memorable brunch dish. If you prefer, you can make one large batch and slice it when cooked.

INGREDIENTS

1lb (450g) large baking potatoes, baked in their skins

4 tbsp olive oil

4 medium leeks, washed and shredded

1 garlic clove, crushed

¾ cup (150g) red kidney beans, soaked overnight and cooked (see page 41)

½ tsp ground coriander

2oz (50g) Cheddar

salt and freshly ground pepper

freshly grated nutmeg

1 egg, beaten

1 tbsp cornstarch

fresh cilantro leaves, to garnish

FOR THE MOJO

4 tbsp chopped fresh cilantro

¾lb (350g) ripe yellow tomatoes, chopped

1 small red onion, chopped

1 green chili, seeded and chopped

1 tbsp red wine vinegar

1 tbsp lime juice

1 For the mojo, combine all the ingredients in a bowl and chill in the refrigerator until required.

2 Scoop out the flesh of the potatoes and crush with a fork. Discard the skins. Heat half the olive oil in a skillet and sauté the leeks and garlic over medium heat for 5 minutes, until soft and lightly browned. Add the kidney beans and cook for 2–3 minutes.

3 Remove from the heat. Mix in the potato, coriander, and Cheddar. Season with salt, pepper, and nutmeg. Transfer to a bowl. Mix in the egg and cornstarch, then cover and chill for 30 minutes.

4 Form the mixture into eight patties. Heat the remaining oil in a skillet and cook the patties over high heat for 6 minutes on each side, until golden. Serve two per person, with the mojo on the side. Garnish with cilantro.

Preparation & cooking time
2½ hours, plus overnight soaking time

Serves 4

Nutritional notes
calories 638; protein 24g; carbohydrates 100g; total fat 19g, of which saturated fat 5g; fiber 15g; sodium 251mg

PERSIAN BAKED EGGS

Guaranteed to wake you up, this spicy egg and tomato dish can be on the table in 20 minutes. Serve with plenty of bread for mopping up the delicious juices.

INGREDIENTS

6 tbsp vegetable oil

2 garlic cloves, crushed

2 green chilies, seeded and chopped

2lb (750g) tomatoes, peeled, seeded, and finely chopped (see page 39)

salt

4 eggs

4 tbsp chopped fresh cilantro, to garnish

pita bread, to serve

1 Heat the oil in an ovenproof skillet, add the garlic and chilies, and sweat for 4–5 minutes over medium heat. Add the chopped tomatoes and cook over low heat until they are reduced to half their quantity and are quite pulpy. Season with salt.

2 Reduce the heat, then carefully crack the eggs into four separate areas of the pan without breaking the yolks. Cover the pan and bake in the oven for 5–6 minutes, or until the eggs are cooked to your taste.

3 Place one egg on each of four plates, divide the tomato mixture among them, and garnish with cilantro. Serve with some warmed pita bread on the side.

Oven preheated to 350°F/180°C

Preparation & cooking time 20 minutes

Serves 4

Nutritional notes calories 336; protein 12g; carbohydrates 20g; total fat 24g, of which saturated fat 4g; fiber 2g; sodium 325mg

EGG QUESADILLAS WITH CHILI POTATOES

This dish gives a new twist to eggs for breakfast. Here they are served Mexican style, all wrapped up in tortillas, with chili-spiced potatoes and a delicious yellow tomato salsa.

INGREDIENTS

4 tbsp oil

¼lb (150g) new potatoes, boiled, peeled, and sliced

1 green chili, seeded and very finely chopped

4 scallions, finely chopped

2 tbsp (25g) butter

4 tbsp heavy cream

1 cup (50g) fresh spinach, cooked and finely chopped

3 eggs, beaten

salt and freshly ground pepper

pinch of freshly grated nutmeg

4 flour tortillas

¾ cup (75g) coarsely grated Cheddar

cilantro leaves, to garnish

FOR THE SALSA

½lb (250g) yellow tomatoes, quartered

1 shallot, chopped

2 tbsp fresh cilantro, chopped

1 green chili, halved and seeded

2 tbsp maple syrup

juice of ½ lime

½ garlic clove

1 For the salsa, place all the ingredients in a blender or food processor and blend to a coarse puree. Season, pour into a bowl, and set aside.

2 Heat the oil in a skillet and sauté the potatoes over fairly high heat for 5–8 minutes until golden, turning them often. Add the chili and scallions, season to taste, remove from the heat, and keep warm.

3 In a large pan, bring the butter and cream to a boil. Reduce the heat, add the spinach and eggs, and cook over low heat, stirring, until you have fluffy scrambled eggs. Add salt, pepper, and nutmeg, to taste.

4 Heat the tortillas in a dry skillet over low heat for 5–10 seconds on each side. Divide the potatoes and eggs among the tortillas. Sprinkle the Cheddar on top. Roll up each tortilla loosely. Cut in half, place on a bed of salsa, and garnish with cilantro.

Preparation & cooking time 40 minutes

Serves 4

Nutritional notes calories 553; protein 17g; carbohydrates 49g; total fat 34g, of which saturated fat 14g; fiber 3g; sodium 520mg

ALFRESCO EATING

COOKING AND EATING OUTDOORS require some special thought. Barbecued food has to stand up to being cooked quickly over an intense heat, while picnic fare must be at its best served cold. Here are some ideas for alliances of vegetables, sauces, and marinades that are accentuated by the wonderful smoky flavors created by barbequing. There are also recipes for picnic foods, such as savory pies and pizza with a salad topping. Mix and match the recipes to suit your needs and the occasion.

——— GRILLED VEGETABLE BARBECUE PITA PIZZAS ———

Grilled Vegetable Pita Pizza

Spinach & Mushroom Pita Pizza

Fennel & Mozzarella Pita Pizza

The variations for toppings on these little pizzas are endless. Here are three of my favorites, but make the most of a long, hot summer and experiment with toppings of your own.

INGREDIENTS

1 zucchini, sliced
1 red pepper, seeded and quartered
1 small red onion, thinly sliced
6 large tomatoes, seeded and chopped
4 tbsp Zhug Relish (see page 67)
1 garlic clove, crushed
½ cup (125ml) olive oil
8 mini pita breads
5½oz (150g) feta cheese, coarsely grated
salt and freshly ground pepper

1 Place the zucchini, pepper, and onion pieces on skewers that have been soaked in water; baste with oil and season well. Barbecue the vegetables for 25 minutes, turning, until well charred. Remove the skewers.

2 Mix the chopped tomato with the zhug relish. Blend together the garlic and oil and brush over one side of each pita, then spread with the tomato and zhug relish.

3 Arrange the vegetables on the pitas. Top with feta and barbecue for 2–3 minutes. Wrap loosely in foil and barbecue for 2–3 minutes more. Serve hot.

——— VARIATIONS ———

Spinach & Mushroom Pita Pizzas
Heat 2 tablespoons of olive oil and sauté 4 sliced garlic cloves over low heat for 8 minutes. Add ¾ cup (75g) sliced mushrooms and sauté for 3 minutes. Stir in ¼lb (150g) spinach. Add nutmeg and season. Spoon onto the pitas, then top with pine nuts and Parmesan shavings. Barbecue as above.

Fennel & Mozzarella Pita Pizzas
Slice 2 fennel bulbs thinly; baste with 4 tablespoons of olive oil. Bake at 400°F/200°C for 3 minutes. Spread 4 tablespoons of Olivada (see page 45) over the pitas, then top with the fennel, 2 thinly sliced zucchini, and 6 sliced sun-dried tomatoes. Brush with olive oil and top with mozzarella. Barbecue as above.

 **Preparation & cooking time**
1 hour

 Serves 4

 Nutritional notes
calories 671; protein 15g; carbohydrates 53g; total fat 46g, of which saturated fat 11g; fiber 5g; sodium 1020mg

FOIL-GRILLED FETA WITH ONION JAM

Feta has the advantage that it keeps its shape well when grilled, so it is perfect for barbecues. You could alternatively use haloumi, another firm-textured cheese. The onion jam keeps well in the refrigerator for three to four days and can be served as a relish with all sorts of dishes. I like to serve it in sandwiches with a grilled vegetable or a cheese base.

INGREDIENTS

7oz (200g) package feta
½ cup (100ml) olive oil
2 garlic cloves, roughly chopped
1 tsp roughly chopped fresh rosemary
1 tsp roughly chopped fresh thyme
1 tsp roughly chopped fresh oregano
salt and roughly cracked black pepper

FOR THE ONION JAM

4 tbsp olive oil
2 medium red onions, chopped
1 tbsp brown sugar
¼ cup (100ml) sherry or red wine vinegar
pinch of ground cumin

1 Cut the feta into four equal slices and place in a large, shallow dish in one layer. Pour the oil over the feta, scatter the garlic and herbs on top, and season with salt (not too much because the feta is already quite salty) and some roughly cracked black pepper. Cover and let marinate in a cool place for up to 4 hours.

2 Meanwhile, for the onion jam, heat the oil over a low heat, add the onion, and cook slowly for 10–12 minutes, until soft and tender. Stir in the remaining ingredients and cook for 30 minutes longer, stirring occasionally, until the onions become soft and syrupy. Remove from the heat and set aside.

3 Remove the feta from the marinade. Lay four pieces of foil, each about 10 inches (25cm) square, out on a table. Divide the onion jam equally between the squares. Top each with a slice of feta and pour 1 tablespoon of the marinade over each piece of feta.

4 Bring the corners of the foil together and fold the top over to encase the onions and cheese. Place the packages on a hot barbecue and cook for 4–5 minutes, until the cheese softens. Transfer to individual plates. Allow guests to open their own pouches so that they can savor the heady aroma that is released.

Preparation & cooking time
1¼ hours, plus 4 hours marinating time

Serves 4

Nutritional notes
calories 497; protein 9g; carbohydrates 11g; total fat 46g, of which saturated fat 12g; fiber 1g; sodium 824mg

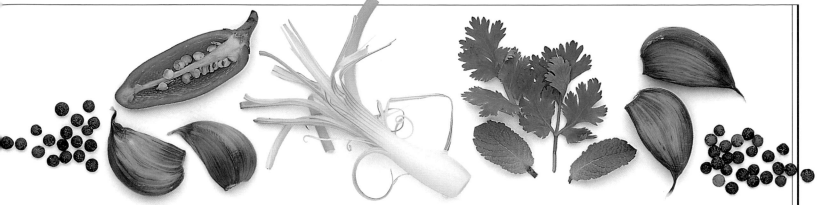

LENTIL BURGERS WITH TOMATO RAITA

I am not usually impressed with vegetarian dishes that imitate meat, but these burgers are in a class of their own. Spiced with chili, cumin, and coriander, and served with a cooling tomato and yogurt sauce, this is one of those dishes that tends to be enthusiastically consumed by nonvegetarians, too. Twice-cooked Spicy Potato Skins (see page 150) make an excellent accompaniment to this dish.

INGREDIENTS

6 tbsp vegetable oil
1 cup (175g) baby lentils, cooked (see page 41)
1 green chili, seeded and chopped
1 garlic clove, crushed
3 scallions, finely sliced
1 tbsp ground cumin
½ tbsp ground coriander
4 tbsp chickpea flour
1 small egg, beaten
4 soft rolls
1 avocado
juice of ½ lemon
salt and freshly ground pepper

FOR THE TOMATO RAITA

6 tbsp plain yogurt
2 tomatoes, cubed
½ tbsp chopped fresh mint
1 tbsp chopped fresh cilantro
2 scallions, finely sliced

1 Heat 4 tablespoons of vegetable oil in a skillet. Add the lentils, chili, and garlic, and cook for 2–3 minutes over medium heat, stirring. Add the onions and spices, and season. Stir in the chickpea flour and cook for 2–3 minutes. Place the mixture in a bowl and let cool.

2 When cool, mix in the egg and stir well to bind all the ingredients together. Cover and refrigerate for 1 hour.

3 Meanwhile, for the raita, blend together all the ingredients in a bowl and season. Cover and let chill in the refrigerator until ready to serve.

4 Take the lentil mixture out of the refrigerator and shape into small burgers or patties. Brush them all over with the remaining oil and grill on a hot barbecue for 3–4 minutes on each side until well browned and sizzling. Alternatively, cook the burgers over high heat for 3–4 minutes on each side.

5 Cut the rolls in half and toast the sliced side for a few minutes on the barbecue. Peel and pit the avocado and slice it thinly. Sprinkle the slices with a little lemon juice to prevent them from discoloring.

6 Place a hefty spoonful of raita on the side of the roll toasted, put a lentil burger on top with a few slices of avocado, then top with the other half of the roll and serve.

🕐 **Preparation & cooking time**
1 hour 50 minutes

◎ **Serves 4**

♡ **Nutritional notes**
calories 694; protein 24g; carbohydrates 82g; total fat 33g, of which saturated fat 6g; fiber 6g; sodium 812mg

PEPPERED MUSHROOM & TOFU SATAY

Mushrooms and tofu work well together on kabobs because they soak up the spicy flavors of the marinade. Here they are served with a peanut vinaigrette, but if you prefer a more traditional satay sauce, try the Asian Peanut Dip (see page 156).

Peppered Mushroom & Tofu Satay

INGREDIENTS

¾lb (350g) firm tofu, cut into 1 inch (2.5cm) chunks
12 large mushrooms, quartered
salt
1 tsp mixed peppercorns, cracked

FOR THE MARINADE

1 stalk lemongrass, chopped
1 tbsp ground cumin
1 tbsp ground turmeric
2 garlic cloves
2 inch (5cm) piece of fresh ginger, grated
2 shallots
½ tsp ground cinnamon
¼ cup (75g) light brown sugar
⅔ cup (150ml) peanut oil

FOR THE PEANUT VINAIGRETTE

6 tbsp (90ml) rice wine vinegar
1 tbsp chopped fresh cilantro
3 fresh mint leaves, chopped
½ garlic clove, crushed
½ red chili, seeded and finely chopped
¼ cup (25g) dry roasted peanuts, chopped
1 tbsp maple syrup
soy sauce, to taste

1 Thread the tofu and the mushroom pieces alternately onto eight wooden skewers that have been soaked in water. Lay the skewers in a shallow dish. Sprinkle with salt and the cracked, mixed peppercorns.

2 For the marinade, place all the ingredients in a blender or food processor and blend to a fine pulp. Pour the marinade over the tofu and mushrooms to coat well. Cover and marinate in the refrigerator for 12 hours.

3 When ready to serve, remove the skewered vegetables from the dish and pat away the excess marinade with paper towels. Place the skewers on the hottest part of the barbecue and cook for 5–8 minutes. Turn the skewers occasionally.

4 Meanwhile, for the peanut vinaigrette, whisk together all the ingredients, and season to taste. To serve, spoon a little peanut vinaigrette onto four plates and place two skewers of vegetables on each plate.

--- VARIATION ---

Eggplant, Potato & Squash Satay
Cook ½lb (200g) large new potatoes in salted, boiling water for 15–20 minutes, until just tender. Drain, and let cool. Peel the potatoes, cut in large chunks, and cut 8 baby eggplants in half, lengthwise. Arrange the potatoes and eggplants with 8 mixed yellow and green pattypan squash in alternate pieces on the skewers. Place the kabobs in 1 batch of prepared marinade (see left). Marinate for 12 hours. Cook on a hot barbecue for 10–15 minutes, turning regularly, until the vegetables are tender. Chop 1 green chili and sprinkle it over the kabobs. Serve with peanut vinaigrette (see above).

Preparation & cooking time
35–40 minutes, plus 12 hours marinating time

Serves 4

Nutritional notes
calories 546; protein 11g; carbohydrates 27g; total fat 45g, of which saturated fat 9g; fiber 1g; sodium 233mg

Eggplant, Potato & Squash Satay

VEGETABLE SHASHLIKS ON TABBOULEH

You can use just about any vegetable to make these kabobs, but for maximum visual appeal it is best to go for a good selection of colors. The beauty of this recipe is that you can vary the flavors by changing the marinade as you wish. I have included four of my favorite marinades to use over a long hot summer.

INGREDIENTS

1 cauliflower, cut into florets and blanched
3 peppers (1 red, 1 green, 1 yellow), cut into 1 inch (2.5cm) chunks
2 zucchini, cut into chunks
¼lb (100g) mushrooms
1 large red onion, cut into wedges

FOR THE TABBOULEH

2 cups (325g) bulgur, soaked in water for 45 minutes and drained
3 tbsp chopped fresh parsley
2 onions, chopped
2 tbsp chopped fresh mint
½ cucumber, chopped
½ cup (100ml) olive oil
juice of 3 lemons
3 tomatoes, peeled, seeded, and chopped (see page 39)
1 batch marinade (see below)

1 Thread alternate pieces of vegetables decoratively onto eight wooden skewers that have been soaked in water. Place them in a shallow dish.

2 Prepare the marinade of your choice (see below). Pour the marinade over the vegetables. Cover and marinate for 1 hour.

3 Meanwhile, for the tabbouleh, place the bulgur in a dish towel and squeeze out any excess water. Transfer the bulgur to a bowl, add the remaining ingredients, and mix well. Season to taste and place in a flat serving dish.

4 Take the skewered vegetables out of the marinade, let any excess drip off, then grill on a hot barbecue for 10–12 minutes, turning regularly, until lightly charred on all sides and cooked through. Arrange the shashliks on the tabbouleh.

5 Gently heat the marinade in a small pan until just before boiling. Pour the marinade over the kabobs to serve. If using the Spicy Yogurt Marinade, do not heat the marinade.

Preparation & cooking time
50 minutes, plus 1 hour for the marinade, plus 1 hour marinating time

Serves 4

Nutritional notes
calories 1001; protein 18g; carbohydrates 87g; total fat 66g, of which saturated fat 9g; fiber 8g; sodium 198mg

Vegetable Shashliks

VEGETABLE SHASHLIK MARINADES

Greek Marinade

Middle Eastern Marinade

GREEK MARINADE
Whisk together ½ cup (100ml) olive oil and the juice of 2 lemons. Stir in 2 crushed garlic cloves, 2 finely chopped onions, 1 bay leaf, and 1 tablespoon of chopped fresh oregano. Let marinate for 1 hour, then use as directed above.

MIDDLE EASTERN MARINADE
Blend ⅔ cup (150ml) olive oil with 2 tablespoons of tomato paste, the juice of 1 lemon, 1 crushed garlic clove, 1 grated onion, and a pinch each of saffron and ground cumin. Mix well, let marinate for 1 hour, then use as directed above.

MOROCCAN MARINADE
Blend ⅔ cup (150ml) olive oil with 1 tablespoon of canned harissa, 1 tablespoon of caraway seeds, a pinch each of cumin and turmeric, and 1 crushed garlic clove. Mix well, then let marinate for 1 hour. Use as directed above.

SPICY YOGURT MARINADE
Blend ⅔ cup (150ml) plain yogurt with 2 tablespoons curry paste, ½ teaspoon ground turmeric, and 1 inch (2.5cm) piece of fresh ginger, grated. Let marinate for 1 hour, then use as directed above, but do not heat this marinade before using.

HOT CHILI-BASTED CORN ON THE COB

Corn on the cob is one of the great treats of summer, even more so when spiked with lots of chili and my favorite herb — cilantro.

INGREDIENTS

6 tbsp olive oil

2 tbsp chopped fresh cilantro

1 tbsp tomato paste

2 tbsp hot chili sauce

4 corn on the cob, husks removed

butter, to serve

fresh cilantro leaves, to garnish

1 For the marinade, whisk the oil, cilantro, tomato paste, and chili sauce in a bowl.

2 Cut each corn on the cob widthwise into three and blanch in a pot of boiling water for about 2 minutes. Drain, then place in a shallow dish. Pour the marinade over the corn to coat well. Cover and leave for 2 hours.

3 Grill the corn on a hot barbecue for 30–40 minutes, regularly turning and brushing with the marinade. Serve hot, topped with butter or more of the marinade. Garnish with cilantro.

Preparation & cooking time
50 minutes, plus 2 hours marinating time

Serves 4

Nutritional notes
calories 338; protein 5g; carbohydrates 24g; total fat 25g, of which saturated fat 7g; fiber 2g; sodium 401mg

TWICE-COOKED SPICY POTATO SKINS

I have never understood why some people throw away the skins from their potatoes: for me this is the tastiest part. When cooked in an Asian-style spice mix, deep-fried potato skins are just irresistible. Try dipping these into sour cream or Tomato Raita (see page 147).

INGREDIENTS

6 large baking potatoes

½ cup (50g) chickpea flour or plain flour

1 tsp turmeric

1 tsp chili powder

½ tsp garam masala

salt

vegetable oil, for frying

1 Prick the potatoes all over with a fork and bake for 1–1¼ hours, depending on their size, until cooked through. Set aside until cool enough to handle.

2 Cut each potato in half lengthwise and scoop out most of the flesh, leaving a ¼ inch (5mm) shell.

3 Cut each skin in half again lengthwise. Mix together the flour, spices, and salt, to taste. Dip the skins in the flour to coat.

4 Heat the oil in a deep-fat fryer or large pan until hot. Fry the potato skins for 3–4 minutes, or until they are crisp. Drain on paper towels, season with salt, and serve.

Oven preheated to
400°F/200°C

Preparation & cooking time
1½–2 hours

Serves 4

Nutritional notes
calories 311; protein 6g; carbohydrates 38g; total fat 16g, of which saturated fat 2g; fiber 4g; sodium 116mg

CHAR-GRILLED TOMATOES WITH GARLIC

Everything tastes good when it has been cooked on a barbecue, and for me tomatoes are no exception. Here basil, garlic, and an open grill combine to give an extra flavor dimension.

INGREDIENTS

4 tbsp olive oil

1 garlic clove, crushed

2 tbsp chopped fresh basil

pinch of superfine sugar

8 ripe but firm tomatoes, halved vertically

salt and freshly ground pepper

1 In a bowl, mix together the olive oil, garlic, basil, sugar, and seasoning until well blended.

2 Place the tomato halves cut-side up on a baking sheet and drizzle the garlic and basil oil over them. Transfer the tomatoes to a hot barbecue and grill for about 8 minutes until charred and softened. Serve hot.

Preparation & cooking time
15 minutes

Serves 4

Nutritional notes
calories 131; protein 1g; carbohydrates 6g; total fat 12g, of which saturated fat 2g; fiber 2g; sodium 114mg

GREEN OLIVE & ONION BREAD

Olives and onions make this loaf hearty enough to serve as the centerpiece of a simple outdoor meal. It is best eaten fresh from the oven, but will still taste great the next day. It is excellent served with cheese.

INGREDIENTS

4 tbsp olive oil, plus extra, to grease
2 onions, chopped
4 cups (450g) unbleached white flour
2 cups (225g) whole wheat flour, plus extra, to dust
1 envelope active dry yeast
2 tsp salt
2 cups (450ml) lukewarm water
1½ cups (200g) pitted green olives, chopped

1 Heat 1 tablespoon of the olive oil in a pan and cook the onions for 5 minutes, until softened; cool.

2 Place both flours in a mixing bowl and stir in the yeast and salt. Pour in 2 tablespoons of oil and slowly add enough lukewarm water to make a soft, but not sticky, dough. You may need to add a little more flour or water to achieve the right consistency.

3 Turn out the dough onto a lightly floured work surface and knead until smooth and elastic.

Place the dough in a large, lightly greased bowl, cover with a clean cloth, and leave in a warm place for 1 hour, until doubled in size.

4 When risen, punch down the dough, turn it onto a lightly floured surface, and knead again for 1 minute. Next, add the cooled onion, the remaining oil, and the olives, kneading again for 2 minutes to combine and distribute the ingredients evenly.

5 Shape the dough into a free-form round loaf, place on an oiled baking sheet, and cover with a clean cloth. Leave in a warm place to rise for 25–30 minutes, until doubled in size.

6 Remove the cloth and bake the loaf for 45 minutes. Tap the bottom to see if it is cooked: it should sound hollow. If it does not, place the loaf back in the oven and bake for a few more minutes until it is done. Cool on a wire rack.

Oven preheated to 350°F/180°C

Preparation & cooking time 1¼ hours, plus 1½ hours rising time

Serves 4

Nutritional notes calories 564; protein 15g; carbohydrates 91g; total fat 18g, of which saturated fat 3g; fiber 6g; sodium 2114mg

LIME-GRILLED FRUIT ON LEMONGRASS STICKS

Barbecuing fruit on lemongrass passes a delicate citrus flavor on to the fruit. You may want to vary the fruit, but this is an exotic, yet simple, kabob to impress your guests. You may need to sharpen the ends of the lemongrass stalks to spear the fruit.

INGREDIENTS

¼ melon of your choice (cantaloupe or Galia), seeded and cut into 1 inch (2.5cm) chunks
1 papaya, cut into 1 inch (2.5cm) chunks
2 plums, halved and pits removed
1 nectarine, cut into 1 inch (2½cm) chunks
12 strawberries
4 stalks lemongrass, tips sharpened
tangy fruit sorbet, to serve (optional)

FOR THE MARINADE

4 tbsp freshly squeezed lime juice
3 tbsp peanut oil
2 tbsp maple syrup
2 tbsp vodka (optional)

1 Whisk together the marinade ingredients. Place all the fruit in a bowl and pour on the marinade. Cover and leave for up to 1 hour in a cool place.

2 Remove the fruit from the marinade with a slotted spoon, then spear alternate chunks onto the lemongrass stalks. Reserve the marinade.

3 Grill the fruit over hot coals for 5–8 minutes, turning and basting them regularly with the marinade until golden and lightly singed. Serve hot from the grill with a tangy fruit sorbet, if desired.

Preparation & cooking time 20 minutes, plus 1 hour marinating time

Serves 4

Nutritional notes calories 269; protein 2g; carbohydrates 45g; total fat 8g, of which saturated fat 2g; fiber 2g; sodium 39mg

CARROT & BEAN PIE WITH THYME CREAM

Lots of fresh thyme and Dijon mustard lift the flavor of simple vegetables in this substantial pie. Served cold, it is a good choice for a picnic or buffet party, and cuts into colorful slices.

INGREDIENTS

butter, to grease
1 batch Short Crust Pastry (see page 42)
6 large carrots
1lb (400g) green beans
1¼ cups (300ml) heavy cream
2 tbsp Dijon mustard
4 tbsp fresh thyme leaves
2 tbsp cornstarch, mixed to a paste with 4 tbsp cold water
6 small eggs, beaten
salt and freshly ground pepper

1 Lightly grease a 8 inch (20cm) springform cake pan. Roll out two thirds of the pastry on a lightly floured work surface and use to line the pan.

2 Cook the carrots whole in boiling, salted water for 10 minutes, until tender; drain.

Slice lengthwise into ⅛ inch (3mm) thick slices. In a separate pot, cook the beans in boiling, salted water for 4 minutes, until al dente. Refresh in cold water, then pat dry.

3 In a small pot, bring the cream, mustard, and thyme to a boil. Stir in the cornstarch paste to thicken the mixture. Let cool, then mix in the eggs.

4 Lay half the carrots in the pastry shell, then lay all the beans over them, and top with the remaining carrots. Press each layer down lightly, season, and pour on a little thyme cream before adding the next layer.

5 Roll out the remaining pastry to cover the pie. Brush the edges with water and press down to seal. Bake for 1¼ hours, until golden. Let rest for 10–15 minutes before slicing.

Oven preheated to 375°F/190°C

Preparation & cooking time 2 hours, plus 40 minutes for the pastry

Serves 10

Nutritional notes calories 874; protein 14g; carbohydrates 71g; total fat 61g, of which saturated fat 37g; fiber 4g; sodium 351mg

VEGETABLE PICNIC CAKE

A cake made with ingredients that are usually associated with savory dishes is not unusual — consider how popular carrot cake has become. Zucchini, sun-dried tomatoes, and pine nuts all have a subtle sweetness, and combine to produce a moist, flavorful cake. Salting the zucchini extracts the excess moisture.

INGREDIENTS

1 cup (175g) coarsely grated zucchini
4 eggs
11 tbsp (150g) unsalted butter, melted
1 tsp vanilla extract
¾ cup (175g) superfine sugar
1⅔ cups (200g) all-purpose flour
1 tsp salt, plus extra, for salting
1½ tsp baking powder
¾ cup (50g) sun-dried tomatoes, sliced
3 tbsp (50g) pine nuts
zest of 1 lemon

1 Place the zucchini in a bowl, sprinkle with salt, and let stand for 10 minutes. Rinse the zucchini under cold, running water, then wrap in a clean cloth and gently squeeze dry; set aside.

2 In a blender or food processor, blend together the eggs, melted butter, vanilla, and sugar. Mix together the flour, salt, and baking powder in a separate bowl, then add to the egg mixture and blend until smooth. Place in a bowl and add the zucchini, sun-dried tomatoes, pine nuts, and lemon zest.

3 Butter and lightly flour an 8 x 4 x 2½ inch (450g) loaf pan. Pour the mixture into the pan, level the top with a spatula, and bake for 10–12 minutes. Reduce the oven temperature to 350°F/180°C and bake for 50 minutes longer. When done, a fine skewer inserted into the middle of the cake should come out clean. Cool on a wire rack.

Oven preheated to
400°F/200°C

Preparation & cooking time
1½ hours

Serves 8

Nutritional notes
calories 394; protein 7g; carbohydrates 43g; total fat 22g, of which saturated fat 12g; fiber 0.2g; sodium 443mg

SPRING VEGETABLE QUINOA

A South American grain, quinoa is packed full of essential nutrients. Its flavor is quite bland, but here it is perked up with an onion-scented herb dressing to make a healthy and refreshing salad.

INGREDIENTS

1½ cups (200g) quinoa
¼ lb (100g) zucchini, thinly sliced
¼ lb (100g) sugar snap peas
½ cup (75g) frozen peas, defrosted
¼ cup (75g) frozen fava beans, blanched and peeled
¾ cup (125g) canned corn kernels
1 red onion, finely chopped
1 stalk lemongrass, finely chopped

FOR THE DRESSING

⅔ cup (50ml) olive oil
1 garlic clove, crushed
1 tbsp white wine vinegar
1 tbsp chopped fresh cilantro
1 tbsp chopped fresh mint
1 tsp ground cumin
salt and freshly ground pepper

1 Place the quinoa in a pan. Cover with cold, salted water, bring to a boil, then simmer for 10–12 minutes. Drain well and let cool.

2 Cook the zucchini and sugar snap peas in boiling, salted water for 2 minutes. Add the peas and beans and boil for 30 seconds longer. Refresh in cold water, then drain.

3 Place all of the ingredients for the dressing in a blender or food processor and blend until smooth. Put the drained quinoa, the blanched vegetables, and the corn in a bowl with the onion, lemongrass, and dressing. Mix the ingredients well and chill in the refrigerator before serving.

Preparation & cooking time
40 minutes

Serves 4

Nutritional notes
calories 642; protein 13g; carbohydrates 58g; total fat 41g, of which saturated fat 6g; fiber 4g; sodium 372mg

CRISP ITALIAN TART

This light tart is quick to assemble and looks very attractive with its colorful rows of contrasting vegetables. You could use puff pastry instead of phyllo pastry, if you prefer.

INGREDIENTS

2 tbsp butter, melted, plus extra, to grease

4 sheets phyllo pastry, each
8 inches x 6 inches (20cm x 15cm)

1 large zucchini

1 large eggplant

4 large plum tomatoes

2 tbsp extra virgin olive oil

1 garlic clove, crushed

salt and freshly ground pepper

1 tsp dried herbes de Provence

1 Lightly grease an 8 inch x 6 inch (20cm x 15cm) baking sheet. Brush each sheet of phyllo with butter and layer the sheets on top of each other on the baking sheet.

2 Slice the zucchini, eggplant, and tomatoes very thin and place on the pastry, overlapping each other, until all the pastry is covered with the vegetables.

3 Mix together the olive oil and garlic and brush over the vegetables. Season with salt and pepper and sprinkle the herbes de Provence over the top.

4 Bake for 10–12 minutes, until the vegetables are tender and the pastry is cooked. Serve the tart either warm or cold.

Oven preheated to 400°F/200°C

Preparation & cooking time 30 minutes

Serves 4

Nutritional notes
calories 166; protein 3g; carbohydrates 11g; total fat 12g, of which saturated fat 5g; fiber 2g; sodium 190mg

MIXED SALAD PIZZA WITH ROASTED GARLIC

Piquant, deliciously creamy Gorgonzola paired with sweet, roasted garlic and the bitterness of salad greens make a superb, rich, and complex topping for a pizza.

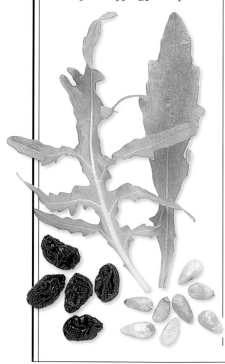

INGREDIENTS

2 cups (225g) unbleached flour, plus extra, to dust

½ tsp fast-acting yeast

pinch of salt

⅔ cup (150ml) lukewarm water

FOR THE TOPPING

2 tbsp olive oil, plus extra, to grease

4 garlic cloves, roasted, peeled, and mashed (see page 50)

7oz (200g) mixed salad greens (arugula, endive, iceberg), shredded

½ cup (75g) raisins, soaked in cold water for 10 minutes, then drained

1¼ cups (150g) grated Gorgonzola

4 tbsp freshly grated Parmesan

2 tbsp pine nuts, lightly toasted

1 For the pizza dough, sift the flour into a large bowl, then stir in the yeast and salt. Make a well in the center of the flour and gradually add the water, mixing the flour in with a wooden spoon to form a soft dough.

2 Knead the dough until smooth and elastic. Place in a lightly oiled bowl, cover with oiled plastic wrap, and let rise in a warm place for 40 minutes, until doubled in size.

3 Meanwhile, for the topping, heat the oil in a skillet, add the roasted garlic and the shredded salad greens, and stir-fry for 5 minutes to wilt the leaves.

4 Place the dough on a lightly floured work surface and punch down with your fists. Knead for 2–3 minutes, then roll out to a circle, about 9 inches (23cm) in diameter and ½ inch (1cm) thick. Place on a greased baking sheet.

5 Roll in the edges of the dough to form the crust. Scatter the raisins over the dough and cover with the garlic and salad greens. Scatter the Gorgonzola, Parmesan, and pine nuts over the top. Bake for 15–20 minutes, until golden.

Oven preheated to 425°F/220°C

Preparation & cooking time 40 minutes, plus 40 minutes rising time

Serves 4

Nutritional notes
calories 646; protein 24g; carbohydrates 63g; total fat 35g, of which saturated fat 11g; fiber 4g; sodium 611mg

*Mixed Salad
Pizza with
Roasted Garlic*

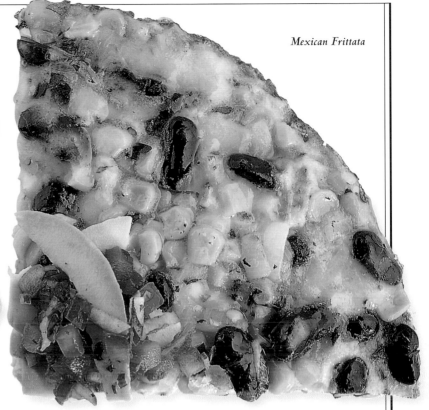

Mexican Frittata

MEXICAN FRITTATA

Flat omelettes, or frittatas, can be filled with all sorts of interesting ingredients — I have gone for a Mexican theme here. The best cooking method is to start the omelette off on the stove and then transfer it to the oven to cook through, as suggested in this recipe. If you do not have an ovenproof skillet, simply cook the omelette on the stove until almost done, then place it under a hot broiler to set the top.

INGREDIENTS

2 tbsp vegetable oil
1 small onion, diced
1 garlic clove, crushed
1 cup (150g) corn kernels
⅔ cup (100g) dried black beans, soaked overnight and cooked (see page 41)
1 tbsp chopped fresh oregano
6 eggs, beaten
salt and freshly ground pepper
2 tbsp unsalted butter
2oz (50g) aged Cheddar
crème fraîche, to serve (optional)

FOR THE AVOCADO SALSA

1 avocado, thinly sliced
½ medium onion, chopped
2 tomatoes, chopped
2 tsp chili sauce
1 tbsp maple syrup
2 tbsp chopped fresh cilantro

1 Place all the salsa ingredients in a bowl. Mix well, then set aside to allow the flavors to develop.

2 Heat the oil in an ovenproof skillet and cook the onion, garlic, corn kernels, and black beans over medium heat for 1–2 minutes. Stir in the oregano, then transfer the mixture to a large bowl. Let cool, then stir in the eggs and season.

3 Melt the butter in the same pan. When melted, return the egg mixture to the pan and cook for 1–2 minutes over low heat, until set around the edges.

4 Transfer the pan to the oven for 10–12 minutes. When the mixture has set completely, remove the pan from the oven and scatter the cheese over the top. Brown under a hot broiler for 1 minute. Divide the frittata into four equal portions and place one portion on four individual plates. Top with the salsa and the crème fraîche, if using.

Oven preheated to 350°F/180°C

Preparation & cooking time 1 hour 50 minutes, plus overnight soaking time

Serves 4

Nutritional notes calories 565; protein 24g; carbohydrates 27g; total fat 40g, of which saturated fat 16g; fiber 3g; sodium 396mg

BLACK-EYED PEA HUMMUS

I must confess that this hummus recipe came about by accident, when I ran out of chickpeas one day. I had no option but to prepare it with black-eyed peas; the result was great.

INGREDIENTS

1 cup (175g) dried black-eyed peas, soaked overnight and cooked (see page 41)

3 garlic cloves, crushed

⅔ cup (150ml) tahini (sesame seed paste)

juice of 2–3 lemons

2 tbsp olive oil

1 tbsp chopped fresh parsley, to garnish

pinch of paprika, to serve

1 Drain the beans, reserving the cooking liquid, and set aside a tablespoon of beans for garnishing.

2 Puree the beans in a blender or food processor with 2 tablespoons of the reserved cooking liquid. When ground to a coarse paste, add the garlic and tahini and blend together thoroughly. Last add the lemon juice and blend until the hummus has a rich, creamy, smooth consistency.

3 Place the hummus in a shallow bowl. To serve, pour the oil over the surface, garnish with the parsley and the reserved beans, and sprinkle paprika over the top.

Preparation time
1 hour 15 minutes, plus overnight soaking time

Serves 10

Nutritional notes
calories 163; protein 7g; carbohydrates 8g; total fat 11g, of which saturated fat 2g; fiber 1g; sodium 10mg

ASIAN PEANUT DIP

Peanut butter provides a useful shortcut when making satay-style sauces. For the best flavor, try to find an unsweetened one. Serve this recipe as a dip or as a sauce for vegetable kabobs.

INGREDIENTS

2 tbsp peanut or vegetable oil

2 garlic cloves, crushed

1 small red chili, seeded and chopped

2 tbsp brown sugar

2 tbsp light soy sauce

¾ cup (175g) crunchy peanut butter

1 tbsp lemon juice

½ cup (100ml) coconut milk

salt and freshly ground pepper

1 Heat the oil in a medium pan and cook the garlic and chili for 2–3 minutes over medium heat; add the sugar and soy sauce and stir until the sugar is dissolved.

2 Mix in the peanut butter and lemon juice, stir well, and add the coconut milk. Bring to a boil, reduce the heat, then simmer, stirring constantly, for about 10 minutes, until thickened. Season to taste and serve.

Preparation & cooking time
20–25 minutes

Serves 10

Nutritional notes
calories 142; protein 5g; carbohydrates 5g; total fat 12g, of which saturated fat 2g; fiber 1g; sodium 288mg

MOROCCAN PEPPER & WALNUT DIP

This is very similar to the Spanish Romanesco sauce, which is traditionally served with seafood. However, it is very versatile: it can be used as a sauce or dressing for vegetables when thinned with a little cream. I also serve it as a dip with pita bread or vegetable crudités.

INGREDIENTS

1 cup (125g) walnuts, roasted

1 tbsp cumin seeds

4 red peppers, roasted, peeled, seeded (see page 39), and cut into strips

1 garlic clove, crushed

1 tbsp lemon juice

2 tbsp olive oil

2 tbsp fresh white bread crumbs

1 tsp harissa, or to taste

pita bread, cut into strips, to serve

1 Place the walnuts and cumin in a blender or food processor and blend to a powder. Add the peppers, garlic, and lemon juice to the walnut mixture in the blender and blend to a coarse paste.

2 Add the oil and the bread crumbs and blend to form a thick, smooth sauce. Add harissa to taste, mix well, and chill for up to 1 hour. Serve with strips of warm pita bread.

Preparation time
50 minutes, plus 1 hour chilling time

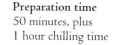

Serves 10

Nutritional notes
calories 222; protein 6g; carbohydrates 25g; total fat 12g, of which saturated fat 1g; fiber 2g; sodium 205mg

CLUB SANDWICH

An American classic, the club sandwich traditionally includes bacon and chicken, and is made with toasted bread. This unconventional vegetarian version is packed full of ingredients with wonderful flavors, such as pesto, goat cheese, roasted peppers, and balsamic vinegar. It proves that tradition need not always be respected when you have imagination.

INGREDIENTS

| 12 slices crusty white bread |
| 2 red peppers, roasted, peeled, seeded (see page 39), and cut into strips |
| 4 hard-boiled eggs, peeled and sliced |
| handful of watercress or arugula leaves |
| 2 plum tomatoes, sliced |
| ¼ cucumber, thinly sliced |
| 1 small red onion, thinly sliced |
| salt and freshly ground pepper |
| 4 tbsp balsamic vinegar |

FOR THE GOAT CHEESE PESTO

| 1 garlic clove, crushed |
| handful of fresh basil leaves |
| 1 tbsp pine nuts |
| ½ cup (100ml) olive oil |
| 1 tbsp freshly grated Parmesan |
| 1½oz (40g) soft mild goat cheese |

1 For the pesto, blend the garlic, basil, and pine nuts to a puree in a blender or food processor, gradually adding the oil as you blend. Add the cheeses, blend, and season.

2 Spread 8 slices of bread thickly with pesto on one side. Lay 4 slices of bread on a work surface, pesto side up. Scatter the peppers over them, followed by the egg and watercress. Top each sandwich with another slice of bread, pesto side up.

3 Arrange a layer of tomatoes, cucumber, and red onion on top. Season, then sprinkle with the vinegar. Top each sandwich with a plain slice of bread. Serve cut into triangles.

Preparation time
50 minutes

Serves 4

Nutritional notes
calories 637; protein 21g; carbohydrates 54g; total fat 39g, of which saturated fat 8g; fiber 4g; sodium 780mg

PAN BAGNAT

Pan Bagnat, which means "bathed bread" in French, is a healthy, filling Provençal sandwich, made with bread moistened with olive oil. Based on the recipe for a Niçoise salad, it is filled with wonderfully colorful ingredients and makes ideal picnic fare. Be sure to use good-quality olive oil for this recipe.

INGREDIENTS

| 4 large rolls |
| 4 garlic cloves, halved |
| 8 tbsp olive oil |
| ½lb (200g) green beans, blanched |
| 4 small tomatoes, quartered |
| 2 small red onions, chopped |
| 16 pitted black olives |
| 6 hard-boiled eggs, quartered |
| 4 small red peppers, roasted, peeled, seeded (see page 39), and cut into strips |
| salt and freshly ground pepper |

FOR THE DRESSING

| ½ cup (125ml) olive oil |
| 4 tbsp balsamic vinegar |
| 1 tbsp chopped fresh basil |

1 Cut the rolls in half, then rub the insides of the rolls with the cut faces of the garlic and brush with oil.

2 Cut the green beans into ¾ inch (2cm) lengths. Place the tomatoes, onions, beans, olives, eggs, and peppers in a bowl. Blend together the oil, vinegar, and basil and drizzle this dressing over the ingredients in the bowl. Toss well and season to taste.

3 Divide the salad ingredients equally among the four roll halves. Top with the remaining roll halves and press down firmly. Serve immediately.

Preparation time
50 minutes

Serves 4

Nutritional notes
calories 743; protein 11g; carbohydrates 42g; total fat 60g, of which saturated fat 9g; fiber 7g; sodium 1183mg

MENU PLANNER

WHEN PLANNING A MEAL, YOU SHOULD
CONSIDER SEVERAL ELEMENTS: THE
NUMBER OF GUESTS, THEIR INDIVIDUAL
TASTES, THE AVAILABILITY OF
INGREDIENTS, AND, MOST IMPORTANTLY,
WHAT YOU ARE HAPPY COOKING.
HERE ARE A FEW SUGGESTIONS TO HELP
MAKE ANY OCCASION — FROM A GARDEN
PARTY TO A FAMILY GET-TOGETHER —
A SUCCESSFUL ONE.

FAMILY-STYLE DINNER

These are wholesome dishes that everyone can
enjoy, followed by an indulgent dessert
that will keep any family happy. Children love
the cheesy crust of the vegetable pie.

CHICKPEA & SWISS CHARD
MINESTRONE WITH PESTO
page 60

ROOT VEGETABLE PIE WITH
POLENTA CRUST
page 88

HAZELNUT TORTE
WITH KIRSCH & BLUEBERRIES
page 126

ABOVE *Root Vegetable Pie with Polenta Crust*
LEFT *Hazelnut Torte with Kirsch & Blueberries*

ONE-POT MEALS

This is an almost effortless way to entertain
your guests. Choose one of these one-pot meals
and serve it with bread and perhaps a salad
for a satisfying lunch or dinner.

MARDI GRAS JAMBALAYA
page 98

CAULIFLOWER & LENTIL PALAK
page 91

VEGETARIAN PAELLA
page 102

RIGHT *Mardi Gras Jambalaya*

WARMING, COMFORTING DINNER

Comfort foods should contain the familiar flavors
of childhood. Cold winter nights were made for
these robust, old-fashioned dishes,
full of soothing carbohydrates.

PARSNIP & WILD RICE
MULLIGATAWNY
page 61

HUNGARIAN STEW
WITH CARAWAY DUMPLINGS
page 96

SWEET OAT TART
page 133

LEFT *Hungarian Stew with Caraway Dumplings*

GARDEN PARTY

Hot summer days demand vibrant tastes
and light dishes that can be prepared in advance.
This menu is perfect for days that are too
hot to spend slaving over the oven.

GRECQUE OF BABY VEGETABLES
WITH HERB CHEESE
page 53

LAZY CARIBBEAN SOUP
page 58

VEGETABLE SHASHLIKS ON TABBOULEH
page 149

CHOCOLATE & CHILI OIL TART
page 130

LEFT *Lazy Caribbean Soup*

LIGHT & HEALTHY

If you are looking for a light meal, but still
want to spoil your guests, try this sophisticated
menu that is low in calories but packed
with extravagant flavors.

HOT & SOUR VEGETABLE SOUP
page 67

POLENTA VERDE WITH
WILD MUSHROOMS
page 105

SAFFRON PEACHES WITH
SUMMER BERRIES
page 124

RIGHT *Saffron Peaches with Summer Berries*

ROMANTIC DINNER

The appetizer and dessert can be prepared in advance, so you can relax and enjoy them with your loved one. The risotto is the only thing that needs last-minute attention.

LAYERED MEDITERRANEAN GATEAU WITH LABNA
page 48

THAI-INSPIRED RISOTTO WITH PUMPKIN
page 101

ITALIAN CREME CARAMEL
page 135

LEFT *Layered Mediterranean Gâteau with Labna*

DINNER PARTY

Dinner with friends should be an informal occasion, when you do not need to stand on ceremony and you can indulge people's tastes or try out unusual recipes.

GOAT CHEESE LATKES WITH BEET SALSA
page 50

CEPE, WALNUT & JERUSALEM ARTICHOKE PACKAGES
page 73

BUTTERNUT SOUFFLE WITH BLACKBERRIES
page 131

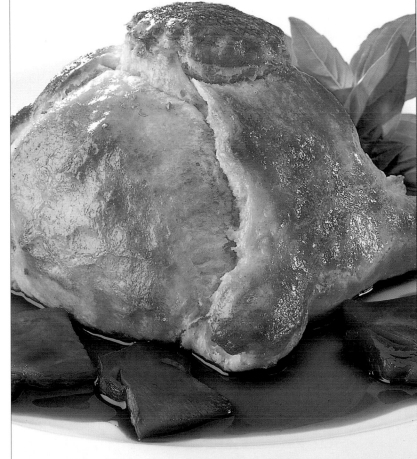

RIGHT *Cepe, Walnut & Jerusalem Artichoke Packages*

BUFFET SUPPER

A buffet table should be generously laden with food, attractively presented, and easy to serve.

CHILI-MARINATED OLIVES, GUACAMOLE
& CHEESE CHALUPAS *pages 56 & 57*

GRILLED VEGETABLE GAZPACHO *page 63*

HIGH-RISE PASTA PIE *page 71*

PURPLE POTATO, ARTICHOKE
& MILLET SALAD *page 122*

SINGAPORE NOODLE SALAD *page 120*

GREEN SALAD
WITH GARDEN HERBS *page 123*

PROSECCO-MASCARPONE &
RASPBERRY SYLLABUB *page 127*

LEFT *Grilled Vegetable Gazpacho*

NEW MED MAGIC

Inspired by the sun-drenched flavors of the Eastern Mediterranean, this spread makes a dazzling summer dinner that tastes best if eaten outdoors.

MIDDLE EASTERN
FLATBREAD & SUMAK SALAD
page 121

GREEK BABY VEGETABLES
WITH ORZO
page 106

CANDIED EGGPLANT
& CARDAMOM ICE CREAM
page 135

RIGHT *Greek Baby Vegetables with Orzo*

SPRING IS IN THE AIR

Spring is a time to serve light dishes using tender young produce such as asparagus, fava beans, and rhubarb. Use simple cooking methods to maximize their fresh flavors.

GRILLED ASPARAGUS
WITH TOPPING
page 51

PENNE WITH BROCCOLI
& FAVA BEAN PESTO
page 82

APPLE & RHUBARB PIZZA WITH
RHUBARB SORBET
page 128

LEFT *Apple & Rhubarb Pizza with Rhubarb Sorbet*

LAZY SUNDAY

Brunch is a relaxed occasion, easy on both the cook and the guests. Serve plenty of champagne and provide the Sunday papers for those who do not like conversation in the morning.

MY FAVORITE MUESLI
page 141

SIMPLE HUEVOS RANCHEROS
page 136

BLUEBERRY PANCAKES
WITH MAPLE SYRUP
page 139

RIGHT *Simple Huevos Rancheros*

163

INDEX

ACKNOWLEDGMENTS

AUTHOR'S ACKNOWLEDGMENTS
The author would like to thank:
My family, for their support and
understanding that a chef's life can
be demanding, hectic, and somewhat
unsociable. Philip Lamb, one of my
Chefs de Partie at the Lanesborough,
who has been instrumental in
helping me test and taste the recipes.
I thank him for his help, support,
and, most importantly, his patience.
Jane Suthering, food stylist, friend,
and respected professional, and

Philip Wilkins, photographer:
this is our second book together and
hopefully not our last. Between them
their expertise never fails to amaze
me. I thank them for bringing the
food to life in their own inimitable
way. Jo Younger, Project Editor, for
her superb editing of my recipes. Her
warmth and good nature, friendship
and patience have been greatly
appreciated. I cannot thank her
enough, and I hope I wasn't too
much trouble. Nicky Vimpany, for

her help also with the editing.
Julia Worth, for her wonderful
design concept for this book, which
I believe brings the whole thing
together in harmony. Danny Murphy
of Chef's Connection, for giving me
such lovely produce to work with on
a daily basis. Jane Middleton, for all
her help. Fiona Lyndsey and Linda
Shanks, my agents, who still manage
to find enough work to fill my spare
time so that I don't get too bored.
Daphne Razazan, Editorial Director

at DK, for giving me the opportunity
to express how interesting and
innovative vegetarian cooking can be.

PUBLISHER'S ACKNOWLEDGMENTS
The publisher would like
to thank: Mary Ling, for initial
editorial planning; Lorraine Turner,
for editorial assistance; Pat Bacon for
nutritional information; Brigid Land,
for photographic assistance;
Emma Patmore, for additional
home economy.